ELK WATCHING

IN PENNSYLVANIA

Elk Watching

in

Pennsylvania

To Joe,
With very best wishes!

Carol J. Mulvihill

Carol J. Mulvihill
12-16-2001

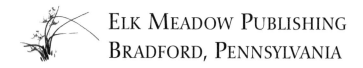

Elk Meadow Publishing
Bradford, Pennsylvania

Published by
Elk Meadow Publishing
38 Nookside Lane
Bradford, PA 16701

Printed by
RJ Communications LLC
51 E. 42nd St. Suite 1202
New York, NY 10017

Design and Layout
HSA Design
4 West 43rd Street
New York, NY 10036

Photography by
Carol J. Mulvihill

Library of Congress Control Number: 2001118645

International Standard Book Number
ISBN 0-9714117-0-0

Printed in the United States of America

Acknowledgments

I owe a debt of gratitude to my husband of twenty-nine years, Michael Mulvihill, who accompanied me on many trips to the Pennsylvania elk range during the past few years. For many months he accommodated my single-minded focus on completing this book, and allowed me to monopolize our computers as well as his home office.

In addition, I thank the following for their assistance in proofreading: Frances Mulvihill and Steve Eidson.

Finally and most of all, I thank God for the inspiration of His Holy Spirit in creating and completing this work.

DEDICATION

I dedicate this book to the memory of John D. Putnam (1922-2001), beloved uncle of my husband Michael. Uncle John lived most of his life in McKean County, Pennsylvania, and had a great love of wildlife and the great outdoors. His children, grandchildren, nephews, and neighbors would always check in at his house to give and to get the latest hunting reports. He loved to listen to everyone's stories, and when he told one of his own, there was always something to be learned.

He graduated from the Ross-Leffler School of Conservation and was a district game protector for the Pennsylvania Game Commission. He was an avid hunter, fisherman, and trapper, and a champion of conservation. In 1980, the National Wild Turkey Federation honored him with the James E. Whilheim Memorial Award.

His tremendous love and commitment to his family during his seventy-nine years was an inspiration to everyone who knew him. He served our country's cause of freedom in the United States Navy during World War II and the Korean Conflict. His commitment to his faith was a powerful testimony to all who spent time with him in his later years. When he died on August 6th, 2001, he was prepared to meet his Lord and Savior, Jesus Christ.

All of his life, Uncle John shared his love and respect for wildlife with everyone around him. Whether he was watching birds and squirrels at the backyard feeder, or hunting deer, turkeys, or black bears, or trapping foxes and coyotes, or watching elk, he loved all the creatures of the Pennsylvania forest. That is why I know he would have enjoyed reading this book.

ABOUT THE AUTHOR

Proud of her Pennsylvania heritage, Carol Mulvihill is a lifelong state resident with a keen interest in the Pennsylvania elk herd. She explains how that interest developed:

"A trip to Yellowstone National Park and the Grand Teton National Park in Wyoming in the summer of 1999 expanded my perspective and appreciation of wildlife and the importance of habitat land in America. I returned from that trip with a renewed appreciation of the elk we have right here in the beautiful forests of Pennsylvania, and a realization that our elk are second to none. My enthusiastic interest in our elk herd rose to new heights, and hasn't subsided since. I realized how blessed we are to have these huge, magnificent creatures inhabiting our forests. And I am happy and thankful to be living in rural Pennsylvania, just 65 miles north of the elk range!"

The Director of Health Services at the University of Pittsburgh at Bradford for 27 years, Carol is a nurse and administrator with a heart of compassion and a creative talent for writing and public speaking. She has delivered numerous professional presentations at annual conferences of the American College Health Association, and was named a Fellow of that organization in 1991. She has published articles in *the Journal of American College Health*, and has authored several health-related articles in *Connections Quarterly for College Health Nurses*, an online publication of which she was editor from 1991 to 2001.

Carol lives in a rustic stone house in Bradford, Pennsylvania with Michael, her husband of 29 years. She is a frequent visitor to the Pennsylvania elk range during every season of the year.

Elk Watching in Pennsylvania is her first book.

CONTENTS

Dedication … … … … … … … … … … … … … … …7
About the Author   … … … … … … … … … … … …9

I: Elk in the Pennsylvania Forests   … … … … … … …17
   Autumn Splendor   … … … … … … … … … … …17
   Home on the Range in Pennsylvania   … … … … …18
   Elk History and Classification   … … … … … … …20
   From Abundance to Extinction   … … … … … …21
   Immigrants from Yellowstone   … … … … … … …23
   The Elk in Benezette   … … … … … … … … …24
   A Second Chance   … … … … … … … … … …25
   Another Wake-Up Call   … … … … … … … … …25
   Brainworm … … … … … … … … … … … … …26
   Herbaceous Habitat: A Healthy Remedy … … … …26
   1982: The Good, the Bad, and the Ugly   … … … …27
   On the Rebound with Continuing Research … … …29
   The Size of the Herd Today   … … … … … … …30

II. The Elk Watching Experience   … … … … … … …31
   Elk Watching: A Growing Pennsylvania Pastime   …31
   The Big Attraction   … … … … … … … … … …33
   Elk Mystique and Bugling … … … … … … … …34
   A Deeper Perspective   … … … … … … … … …35
   Where Are the Elk? … … … … … … … … … …36

Elk Watcher's Code of Conduct 39
    Think: Safety First 39
    Be Respectful of the Elk—
    You are a Guest on Their Home Range 41
    Be Kind, Considerate, and Respectful of
    Residents as Well as Other Tourists 41
    Things to Bring on Your Elk Watching Trip 42
    Things to Leave at Home 42

Part III: The Elk Watcher's Journal 43
First Elk Watching Trips 44
    May 1995
    Carol's First Elk 44
    First Bull Elk on Winslow Hill 45

    June 1999
    First Bulls in Yellowstone 46
    An Increased Appreciation 47
    Elk vs. White-Tailed Deer 47

Springtime Awakening
    April 8, 2001
    Lightheaded Royalty 59
    Keeping Antlers in April 50
    Return to Royal Splendor 51
    Antler Shedding 52
    Antlers of Young Bull Elk 52
    Elk Teeth 53

    April 22, 2001
    Return to Winslow Hill 54
    Weakened Yearlings 54
    Bull Elk Crossing the Bennett's Branch 55
    Talks With Elk 56
    The Elk Lick 57

May 6, 2001
Heaven's Meadow   … … … … … … … … … … … …58
A Yearling Running Sprints … … … … … … … …600

May 10, 2001
The Deal   … … … … … … … … … … … … … … …60
Back to the Peaceful Meadow   … … … … … … …61
Cud Chewing … … … … … … … … … … … … …61
Knuckle Popping   … … … … … … … … … … …61
Just One More Drink   … … … … … … … … … …61
Lazy Grazing Through the Woods … … … … … …62
Looking for Velvet   … … … … … … … … … … …62
Elk on the Playground … … … … … … … … … …63
A Monster Bull in the Making   … … … … … …64
Bachelor Party of Five … … … … … … … … … …65
Baseball, Elk, and Burgers … … … … … … … …82

June 7, 2001
Visitors from Wyoming   … … … … … … … … …82
Sweet Clover in Heaven's Meadow … … … … …83
Matriarch Cows   … … … … … … … … … … … …84
Bulls on Their Own … … … … … … … … … … …84
Expectant Cows   … … … … … … … … … … … …85
Big Bulls in Medix Run   … … … … … … … … …86
Pregnant Cows and Parturition … … … … … …87
Elk Commotion   … … … … … … … … … … … …87
Predators   … … … … … … … … … … … … … …88

June 13, 2001
A Lone Cow Chases Away a Yearling   … … … …88
The Cow Song   … … … … … … … … … … … …89
Bulls in the Ball Field   … … … … … … … … …89

Summer Days

June 25, 2001
Flora and "Fawna" … … … … … … … … … … … ...91
Cowgirls … … … … … … … … … … … … … ...91
Cow Crossing the Bennett's Branch … … … … ...92
Bachelor Group in Medix Run … … … … … … ...93

June 29, 2001
A Wildlife Watching Day … … … … … … … … ...93
Calves in Hiding … … … … … … … … … … … ...94
A Healthy Fear … … … … … … … … … … … … ...94
Stomping, Snorting, Kicking White-Tails … … ...95
Creatures Great and Small … … … … … … … … ...96
The Great Blue Heron … … … … … … … … … ...97
Conversation at the Elk Country Store … … … ...97
Two Broods of Turkeys Crossing the Road … … ...98
Reflections on a Beautiful Day … … … … … … ...98

July 7, 2001
Bulls in Cameron … … … … … … … … … … … ...99
Cows and Butterflies … … … … … … … … … … ...99
Elk Path Processions … … … … … … … … … … ...100

July 14, 2001
Back Together Again … … … … … … … … … … ...101
"Sarah, Plain and Tall" … … … … … … … … ...102
The Cow with Earrings and a Necklace … … … ...102
Wild Turkeys on the Food Plot … … … … … ...103
The Big Bull Downtown … … … … … … … … ...104
Velvet Air-Conditioners … … … … … … … … ...105
Horns vs. Antlers … … … … … … … … … … … ...105
Eli, the Newborn Elk Calf … … … … … … … ...105

August 2001
Gigantic Antlers … … … … … … … … … … … ...106
Rubbing Off theVelvet … … … … … … … … ...107
Sparring … … … … … … … … … … … … … ...108

Autumn Activity

September 2000
Scent Rituals 109
A Pause in the Rut 110
Watching for Elk 112
The Bonfire and the Bugling 112
Mating Behavior 113
Watching Bulls and Their Harems 117
The Bull Elk and the White-Tails 118

October 1, 2000
The Little Mus-Koose 119
Morning Walk with a Monarch 120

October 14, 2000
Rut Winding Down 122
Traffic Hazards on Winslow Hill 123
Colorful Autumn 124

October 24, 2000
Bulls in Camouflage 124
Pheasant in Hiding 125
Three Turkeys Trotting 125

Winterlude

January 2, 2001
Elmer's Elk 125

March 3, 2001
A Lone Bull in Winter 127
Winter Pelage, Wonderfully Made 127
Cows Carrying the Herd 129
Chasing Antler Sheds 130
The Great Antler Auction 130
The Sweet Promise of Springtime 131

Part IV: Issues in Elk Country 133
  Those Blankity-Blank Elk 133
  Forgive Us Our Trespassing 133
  Elk Hunting Reintroduced 134

Part V: Looking to the Future 139
  The Elk Watcher's Wish List 139
  The Pennsylvania Elk Watching
  and Nature Tourism Project 139
  Our Shared Responsibility 140
  What Can You Do for the Elk? 140
  Conservation by Choice, Not by Chance 141

Works Cited 143

I

ELK IN THE PENNSYLVANIA FORESTS

Autumn Splendor

A casual afternoon drive along the country roads of north central Pennsylvania in October provides an unprecedented opportunity to experience the sights, sounds, smells, and feel of autumn in all of its glory. You can view the kaleidoscope colors of the foliage unfolding in the sunlight, and savor the sweet, fresh smell of the brisk autumn air, and the crisp, crackling sound of the dried leaves under your shoes. You can marvel at the silent display of a signature sunset in the Allegheny Mountains. Then, if you are privileged, you will hear the piercing sound of a bugling bull elk resonating through the valley in the fading twilight. As your eyes search the lawns and fields along the sides of the road, you will be left breathless at the sight of one of nature's most splendid and majestic creatures…the elk.

Home on the Range in Pennsylvania

Nestled in the heart of the Allegheny Mountain Plateau of north central Pennsylvania are the wooded forests and rich green meadows which are home to more than 700 wild elk, one of the largest herds east of the Mississippi River. Abandoned coal strip mines have been transformed into herbaceous food plots with lush meadows of alfalfa and clover to support the habitat of the growing Pennsylvania elk herd. In recent years, an ambitious cooperative program was undertaken by the Pennsylvania Game Commission, the Pennsylvania Department of Conservation and Natural Resources, and the Rocky Mountain Elk Foundation to expand the elk range and enhance the habitat. These efforts have been a boon to the health and survival of this magnificent elk herd, which has become a treasured natural resource to many Pennsylvania residents and visitors alike.

The elk range is no game preserve; it is an open range where the elk live and roam freely — much to the chagrin of local farmers and residents whose crops and vegetation are often and repeatedly consumed by these huge, wild, yet usually docile and somewhat timid creatures — and much to the delight of the growing number of elk watchers from within and outside of the state.

A combination of state game lands, state forests, state parks, and private land comprise the 835 square miles of the Pennsylvania elk range. It is located in parts of Elk, Cameron, Potter, Clearfield, Clinton, and Centre counties. The range consists of two parts: the traditional range consisting of approximately 225 square miles and located north of Rt. 555, and the expanded range, adding an additional 610 square miles to the south and east of the traditional range (Cogan, "Elk Hunt").

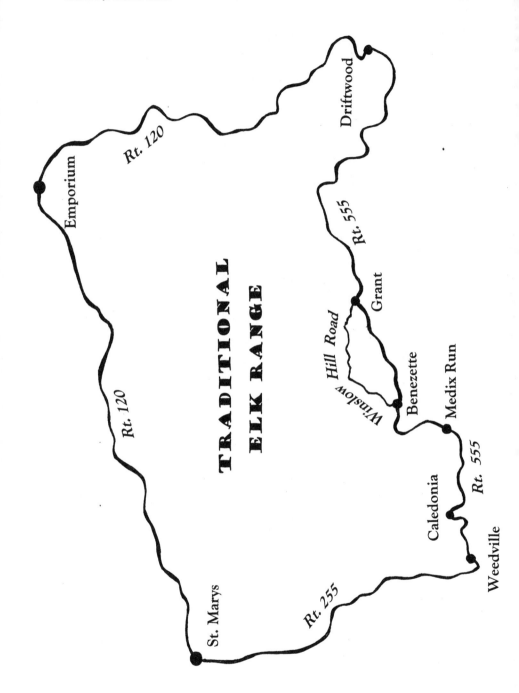

Elk History and Classification

Scientists believe that elk traveled from Asia to the North American continent by way of the Bering Land Bridge during a glacial age, perhaps as many as 100,000 years ago or as recently as the last ice age 10,000 years ago (Furtman 24, 27). For hundreds of years, long before the early settlers from Europe arrived in North America, as many as ten million elk inhabited the land. The herds steadily diminished with the growth of civilization and the development of towns, farms, settlements, and commerce on the continent. By the early part of the 20th century, the elk population had diminished to less than 100,000 (Robb 10). One source stated,"By 1907, it is estimated that only 41,000 elk survived" (Furtman 48). But thanks to effective conservation strategies and wildlife management, the elk population in North America has rebounded to approximately one million animals today, living in twenty-four states and five Canadian provinces (Bishop, "Elk Facts").

Elk are sometimes called "wapiti," a Shawnee word meaning "white rump," one of the elk's distinguishing physical characteristics. In biological classification or taxonomy, elk are members of the genus *Cervus* and of the species *elaphus*, or "red deer." They are one of five species of the North American Deer Family. The four others are moose, caribou, mule deer, and white-tailed deer.

Originally, there were six subspecies of elk in North America. These are their names and the areas they have occupied (Furtman 28-42) :

Eastern elk (Canadensis), which ranged throughout the eastern United States and north into Canada. (extinct)

Manitoban elk (Manitobensis) which once inhabited the Great Plains and now range in parts of Canada.

Merriam's elk (Merriami) which lived in the Southwest states and Mexico. (extinct)

Tule elk (Nannodes) living in central California.

Rocky Mountain elk (Nelsoni) which range throughout the
Rocky Mountains and also live in a number of other
states to which they have been translocated.
Roosevelt or Olympic elk (Roosevelti) living near the coast of
Oregon and Washington, including the Olympic
Peninsula.

The original native subspecies or ecotype of Eastern elk
(*Cervus elaphus canadensis*) occupied land primarily east of the
Mississippi River. Eastern elk populated the land north into
Ontario and southern Quebec, and south into the northern
parts of the southern states, including Georgia, Alabama and
Louisiana (Geist 33). They were numerous in the forests of
Pennsylvania, particularly in the central Allegheny Mountains.

From Abundance to Extinction

In Michael Furtman's *Seasons of the Elk*, reference is made
to a journal article written by Dr. B. S. Barton in 1806, originally published in *Lives of Game Animals* by Ernest Thompson
Seton. The journal entry gives descriptive evidence of the abundance of Eastern elk in Pennsylvania during Barton's lifetime:

> Within the memory of many persons now living,
> the droves of Elks which used to frequent the
> salines west of the river Susquehanna in
> Pennsylvania, were so great that for 5 or 6 miles
> leading to the "licks," the paths of these animals
> were as large as many of the great public roads of
> our country. Eighty Elks have sometimes been seen
> in one herd upon their march to the salines. (qtd in
> Furtman 31)

Olaus Murie, a field naturalist and one of the world's foremost authorities on elk, wrote in his book, The Elk of North
America: "Records indicate that elk at one time roamed over

nearly all parts of Pennsylvania, and that their favorite ranges were in the middle sections of the state, particularly the Allegheny Mountains." (36)

Murie quoted from Richard Gerstell's writings in 1936:

> During the 1840's and up until the early 1850's a
> fair number of elk yarded [gathered together in
> groups] and were annually hunted in those sections
> of Elk, Cameron, and McKean Counties lying
> between the headwaters of Bennett's Branch of the
> Susquehanna on the southeast and the Clarion
> River on the north and west. It was due to the pres-
> ence of these animals in the region that Elk County
> received its name when established in 1843. (qtd in
> Murie 37)

Throughout the eighteenth and nineteenth centuries, elk were hunted extensively and often killed by settlers to stop farm crop consumption, for which elk are still notorious even to this day. The year 1867 marked a tragic occurrence in history when the last Eastern elk (*Cervus elaphus canadensis*) living in Pennsylvania was killed near the Clarion River, bringing this subspecies to extinction according to confirmed reports (qtd in Murie 37). There were also reports of "live specimens seen in Pennsylvania by John G. Hamersley, 'a careful student of wildlife,' in 1869 and 1870" (qtd in Murie 37). Henry Shoemaker wrote of another unconfirmed report that the last two Eastern bull elk were killed in Pennsylvania as late as 1878 (qtd in Murie 37). More important than the dates and details of the final event is the sobering fact that a once plentiful animal subspecies became extinct by the end of the nineteenth century, due to unrestricted hunting, killing of elk by farmers because of crop losses, and decreased habitat land due to the expansion of civilization.

Immigrants from Yellowstone

The elk now living in the forests of north central Pennsylvania are the descendents of Rocky Mountain elk (*Cervus elaphus nelsoni*), majestic immigrants brought here from the West. This subspecies is famous for having the largest antlers of any of the six subspecies of elk of North America (Murie 12). How did these elk end up in Pennsylvania? Believe it or not, they took the train!

Between 1913 and 1926, Pennsylvania imported or purchased a total of 177 elk in an effort to reintroduce the elk population into several areas of the state (Murie 38). The first group of 50 Rocky Mountain elk from Yellowstone National Park in Wyoming were transported by railway to Pennsylvania in 1913, according to "Pennsylvania's Wildlife Conservation History," published by the Pennsylvania Game Commission. Half were released in Clinton county and the other half in Centre county. In addition, according to that report, 22 elk from a private preserve in Pike county were purchased that year; 10 were released on state lands in Monroe county and 12 were placed in a Centre county preserve.

In 1915, another shipment of 95 Yellowstone elk were distributed into six counties: Cameron, 24; Carbon, 24; Potter, 24; Forest, 10; Blair, 7; and Monroe, 6. An Altoona businessman donated a dozen elk in 1918 or 1919. In 1924, 6 elk were purchased from South Dakota, and in 1926, another 4 were purchased from South Dakota ("Pennsylvania's Wildlife Conservation History").

The total number of elk reintroduced or released into the wild in Pennsylvania between 1913 and 1926 was 177, after subtracting the 12 which were placed in a preserve from the 189 total elk acquired according to the records. Immigrants from the West totaled 155, including 145 from Yellowstone and 10 from South Dakota.

The elk from Yellowstone National Park were purchased from the federal government by the Pennsylvania Game

Commission for the mere cost of capturing and transporting them via railroad car, a price of $30 per elk (Kosack). What a deal! At that time, the burgeoning Yellowstone elk population needed to be curtailed due to hard winter conditions and inadequate food supply. Moving some of the elk to other areas of the country was a brilliant strategy of wildlife management implemented by the federal government from 1892 to 1939. A total of 5,210 elk were shipped from Yellowstone to 36 different states (Murie 319). President Theodore Roosevelt, an avid conservationist, hunter and outdoorsman, was supportive of the elk relocation program as well as other outstanding national conservation efforts, such as the establishment of the first National Forest. It was during his term as President of the United States that Pennsylvania purchased the elk from Yellowstone.

Figuratively speaking, the Rocky Mountain elk in Pennsylvania are a rare gift. Initially a bargain at $30 per head, they have become a priceless Pennsylvania treasure as well as an enormous responsibility.

The Elk in Benezette

The elk which now occupy the range in Benezette township in the north central Allegheny Mountains are thought to be the descendants of 24 Yellowstone elk introduced into Cameron county in 1915, 6 bull elk from South Dakota released in 1924, and 4 from South Dakota in 1926 ("Pennsylvania's Wildlife Conservation History").

After the elk got off of the train in Cameron County, some of them roamed and finally settled in the forests of none other than Elk County! I think they read the signs and figured that would be a good place for them to make their home. Over the years, the elk have grown to prefer the area in and around Benezette. They have literally made it their favorite stomping grounds!

Other elk that were reintroduced into eastern and central areas of the state, including the Pocono Mountains and State College area, died out quickly. But the Rocky Mountain elk brought into Cameron County in north central Pennsylvania survived. Their descendants now thrive, interestingly enough, on the same geographic range originally occupied by Pennsylvania's native Eastern elk which became extinct in the late 1800's.

A Second Chance

After one subspecies of elk was lost forever more than a century ago, Pennsylvanians welcomed a second chance to manage elk responsibly. But when hunting of the immigrant elk herd was permitted from 1923 until 1931, 98 bulls were legally killed, and elk hunting was suspended in Pennsylvania. Even after elk hunting was suspended, killing of elk by farmers because of crop losses, and illegal killing of elk continued to occur. The state and the nation had other priorities during and after World War II. The elk in Pennsylvania roamed the wooded wilderness for 40 years without much attention until the early 1970's. The population of the elk herd had dwindled to an estimated remnant of about two dozen by 1940 (qtd in Murie 38), and had grown only to 65 by 1971, the year of the first elk census (Kosack).

Another Wake-Up Call

In 1973, the elk population began another downward shift, reaching a low of 38 in 1974 (Kosack) due to insufficient habitat, crop damage conflicts, illegal killings, and brainworm infection. This wake-up call drew public attention to the elk herd and brought together a variety of agencies to plan solutions to these problems. At the same time, there was an outcry from farmers demanding relief from crop damage inflicted by the elk. Even when the elk population was startlingly low, crop damage complaints and elk killings were high. Farmers needed relief, and the elk herd was in danger of being extinguished. New approaches to resolving crop damage conflicts and the resultant killing of elk had to be forged.

Brainworm

A parasitic disease called brainworm was one cause of the diminished elk population in the early 1970's. It was diagnosed by necropsies performed by wildlife researchers at the Pennsylvania State University. The parasite is carried by snails and slugs, which acquire it from the droppings of white-tailed deer. The slugs carrying the brainworm parasite are accidentally ingested by the elk during grazing. The stringy worm or nematode attacks the brain and central nervous system of the elk, leaving the infected animal deranged, incapacitated, and unable to forage for food, ultimately leading to death. It is an interesting fact that the white-tailed deer in the same area are the primary host of this disease, and although they have the brainworm parasite in their bodies, it does not seem to affect them adversely ("Elk Wildlife Note"). Brainworm took a toll on the elk population in 1973-74. But since then, fewer than five elk deaths from brainworm per year have been identified (Kosack).

Herbaceous Habitat: A Healthy Remedy

Habitat consists of a combination of components including food, water, cover, and space, which populations need to survive and thrive ("Elk Habitat"). Habitat enhancement has undoubtedly improved the health of the herd by providing new and expanded elk feeding areas. Much like good nutrition strengthens the immune system in humans, it is very likely that the addition of herbaceous openings and food plots on the elk range has helped to strengthen the immune system of the elk.

There are a variety of factors which may account for decreased transmission of the brainworm parasite, such as reduction in the population of white-tailed deer on the elk range, and dry summers which decrease the number of slugs in the grasses on which elk feed. There may even be factors not yet considered which may make it possible for the adaptable surviving elk to develop immunity or decreased susceptibility to infection. One thing is certain: the incidence of brainworm infection has diminished. Only with continued elk research can biologists identify and confirm the reasons with certainty.

The habitat enhancement also helped discourage crop damage by luring the elk to food plots planted away from the farmland they had been invading on a regular basis. It didn't eradicate the problem, but it was a step in the right direction.

By 1981, the elk population had rebounded to 135 (Kosack), more than triple the population of 38 estimated in the 1974 census.

1982: The Good, the Bad, and the Ugly

One of the highest mortality years in Pennsylvania's more recent elk history was 1982. The Game Commission announced a plan to reintroducing elk hunting in Pennsylvania and to issue 30 hunting licenses (Kosack). Even before the proposal was finalized, some individuals took matters into their own hands. That year, 15 elk were killed illegally and 11 were killed for damaging crops ("Elk Mortalities 1975-99"). This compared with 1 killed illegally and 6 killings due to crop damage during the previous year. Combined with other known elk deaths, the total mortality was 35 elk in 1982, according to the report. Because of this occurrence, there was no longer a need to further reduce the size of the elk herd and the proposed plan for an elk hunt was eliminated.

The majority of local citizens were outraged at the unlawful and excessive killing of the elk. What was the sense of opposing a legal hunting season, yet killing the elk anyway? Perhaps what occurred was due in part to the strong feelings of frustration on the part of some of the local farmers and a few residents. Some rationalized that since the elk ate their crops and consumed their plants, shrubs, and trees, they should be the ones to kill them, and they shouldn't have to pay for a license to do it. Maybe it was a power play or anger on the part of local farmers against the Game Commission or public authorities in general, which were not providing them with what they thought were adequate solutions and relief for crop damage losses. Whatever the reason, the unlawful and excessive killing of the elk in 1982 was a sad and unfortunate occurrence. Surely people can reason together and work toward solutions without disregard for laws and civility.

But that is past history; those events happened nearly two decades ago. Like a phoenix rising out of the ashes, there was something good born out of those events: a new cooperative elk management plan was enacted by the Pennsylvania Game Commission and the Department of Environmental Resources Bureau of Forestry, and more than 30 acres of food plots were planted on the traditional elk range (Harrison 24). Another generation has passed, and the resilient elk herd is now growing and thriving, both despite and because of some of the events of 1982.

In the decades that followed, the Pennsylvania Game Commission, the Department of Environmental Resources Bureau of Forestry, the Rocky Mountain Elk Foundation, the North Central Pennsylvania Regional Planning and Development Commission, and other agencies worked together to implement an ambitious plan of action to continue to improve habitat, support elk research, resolve conflicts, and protect the herd from unlawful killings. Due largely to the combined efforts of these supporting agencies, the Pennsylvania Rocky Mountain elk (*Cervus elaphus nelsoni*) herd has been successfully reestablished and nurtured.

On the Rebound with Continuing Research

It is no small coincidence that life has been improving for the Pennsylvania elk since Rawley Cogan, a wildlife biologist, began working for the Pennsylvania Game Commission's "Elk Project" in 1982. Throughout the past two decades, his leadership and expertise have been demonstrated in the coordination of many elk project initiatives and research, sometimes in conjunction with other researchers from the Pennsylvania State University, and Frostburg State University, as well as the Rocky Mountain Elk Foundation, Safari Club International, and other organizations.

The annual aerial and ground population survey has been essential in the development of sound elk management objectives and strategies (Cogan, "Survey" 16). Initiation of a trap and transfer project has enabled the capture and relocation of part of the growing elk population to areas on the expanded elk range to the south and east, away from private farmland on the traditional range. The attachment of radio collars or transmitters to elk for the purpose of telemetry monitoring has provided important information about elk movement and range, reproduction, mortality, and calf survival.

Bob Decker, who worked with the elk trap and transfer project, says this about his colleague Rawley Cogan: "He knows more about the elk than the elk know about themselves!" That knowledge enables sound elk management planning and strategies to secure the future of a healthy herd and adequate elk range habitat for the years to come.

According to Cogan, who is now the Chief Wildlife Biologist with the Pennsylvania Game Commission and the state's leading elk expert, the elk herd has experienced steady growth since 1988 ("Survey" 16).

The Size of the Herd Today

Considering the estimated average annual elk population growth increase of 12-16% in Pennsylvania elk, with elk calves born in May and June of 2001, it was anticipated that the elk herd population would reach 700 by the summer of 2001 (Cogan, "Elk Hunt" 17).

An annual elk population aerial and ground survey provides important information for responsible elk management. According to Cogan, a three-day survey conducted in February 2001 estimated the Pennsylvania herd at 622; this compares to 566 the previous year ("Survey" 17).

According to the 2001 Elk Survey (17), the elk population of 622 included 311 adult cows, 106 adult bulls, 56 spike bulls, 135 calves, and 14 of unknown sex and age. The survey reported 50 elk deaths in the year 2000, including 12 by motor vehicles and 6 by trains. Four elk were killed because of crop damage. There were 3 accidental deaths, 2 deaths due to tick infestation and 17 deaths from unknown causes.

In September 2001, Cogan projected that the Pennsylvania elk population could reach 1,054 by 2005.

II

THE ELK WATCHING EXPERIENCE

Elk Watching: A Growing Pennsylvania Pastime

Each year, the enthusiasm for elk watching in Pennsylvania increases. The small country villages of Benezette, Grant, Driftwood, Medix Run, Caledonia and Weedville have become hosts to a growing number of tourists eager to see the majestic elk. A survey conducted by Pennsylvania State University estimated the tourist population at 75,000 in 1999, with approximately 93% of visitors to elk country from within the state, and 65% consisting of family groups ("Visiting Pennsylvania's Elk Range").

People, young and old, and from every walk of life drive through the small country villages along the "Elk Highway," Pennsylvania Rt. 555, looking for elk. Many bring other visitors and family to the range. In recent months, I've met and spoken with numerous visitors to Pennsylvania. On one trip to the elk range, I met a family from Dubois, who brought visiting relatives from Illinois to Benezette to see the elk. Another family from Punxsutawney brought visitors from New Hampshire. A couple of folks were using huge binoculars to scan the landscape from the Scenic Elk Viewing Area on Winslow Hill. They told me that they travel twice a year from Youngstown, Ohio, just to visit the elk range in Pennsylvania. These are examples of the geographic diversity of the tourists I met on a single visit to the elk range at Winslow Hill in April 2001. It also suggests what I suspect is a growing trend: Pennsylvania residents are bringing visitors and family from other areas to see the elk in Pennsylvania.

Enjoying elk or other wildlife as a family is an activity that everyone can usually agree upon. For children, elk watching can be educational as well as fun. Many teens find the elk herd fascinating and like to take their friends on tours. For busy, hard-working adults, a visit to elk country offers an escape from the hectic pace and stress of modern life. Sometimes, folks from the city like to go to the country to "get away from it all." Others find inspiration in nature and wildlife. Hunters enjoy observing wildlife in their natural habitat, particularly big game animals like the elk. Senior citizens enjoy a car trip to elk country because it doesn't require a lot of physical exertion, yet is an interesting outing. Elk watching is an experience people of all ages can enjoy together. For some, it provides an opportunity to do something out of the ordinary. Regardless of the motivating factors, the benefits of relaxation and renewal can be enjoyed by everyone. Even the drive to and from elk country can be refreshing and therapeutic.

On a nice day, a visit to elk country involves a pleasant ride through the Allegheny Mountains in one of the most beautiful states in the country. The air in north central Pennsylvania is so "country fresh" that I wish I could capture it and save it in a zip-lock plastic bag! It might be worth money in smog-filled cities! And I do believe that in the springtime, the peepers sing louder along Pennsylvania Rt. 555 than anywhere else on the face of the earth. For such tiny frogs, they certainly have great lungs and vocal cords. Their symphony can drown out a car radio! Such occurrences inevitably make the drive to and through elk country a refreshing sensory excursion!

The Big Attraction

The colorful Pennsylvania autumn foliage display and the September-October "rut" or mating season of the elk combine to provide a spectacular double feature for visitors and locals alike. The show usually runs for several weeks, with peak performances from late September through early October. Of course, the highlights are the bugling performances by the bull elk and the antler displays and competitions. Actually, the bugling begins as early as the end of August. But if you want the peak foliage as well, a trip during the first or second week in October should still offer the prime time double feature. The popular autumn spectacle draws crowds and traffic to the elk range. If you dislike traffic jams you might plan a mid-week trip or a visit during the spring or summer. Elk country is gorgeous during any season, and the elk are there all the time.

Why are the elk such a big attraction? If you've ever been to Benezette — or to Yellowstone National Park — you know that observing and encountering wildlife in their natural habitat is an exhilarating, often surprising, sometimes scary, and always memorable experience. Elk are such a big attraction partly because they *are* big — *really* big animals — majestic with their enormous antlers, and almost mystical in appearance when shrouded in the early morning mist.

Unlike white-tailed deer, which turn up their white flag-like tails and run when people come near, the elk are not easi-

ly intimidated, and therefore, can often be observed at relatively close range for extended periods of time. This allows
plenty of time for photography, and gives all spectators an
ample opportunity to observe. You might even have time
enough to run and buy more film!

Another great excitement about elk watching is the element of surprise. You will not only find them in the open meadows and forests as you might expect, but also in the lawns by the
camps and buildings where you'd least expect, and sometimes
in or near the roads or crossing the streams. An unexpected
sighting of an 800 pound, large-antlered bull elk "up-close and
personal," at a 10-yard distance, will get your adrenaline flowing and your heart pounding and will literally take your breath
away. Once you make eye contact, you'll be intrigued. Such an
encounter will make you eager to learn more about these magnificent creatures, and eager to return to see them again. When
you do, you won't always find them in the same places where
you saw them the last time. This makes each elk watching experience a unique and unpredictable adventure, and always worth
the trip.

Elk Mystique and Bugling

Elk have a certain intrigue, mystique, and magnetism.
Their stature is huge, their structure is powerful and graceful,
and their massive antlers are ominously impressive.
Paradoxically, their usual calm timidity and large brown cow-
like eyes suggest friendliness and non-aggression...but don't
count on it during the rut, nor during the calving and nursing
season. They are wild animals, and their behavior is sometimes
unpredictable when affected by hormones and bound by natural instincts. Being close to an elk is always thrilling and somewhat scary even to seasoned elk watchers and hunters.

The eerie bugling of the herd bulls in early autumn is a
sound which has been heard each autumn over many centuries
of time by many ears of mankind. Elk inhabited this continent

long before our immigrant ancestors from Europe set foot on North American soil. Native Americans heard the bugling of the elk, with which they shared the land. The elk, or "wapiti," were essential to the lives of many tribes, providing them with food and hides for clothing and shelter, as well as tools, weapons and ornaments. Some tribes, like the Oglala, considered elk sacred ("Elk in History").

During the fall rut or mating season, the bugling of the bull elk serves as a mating call and as a challenge to competitors. The sound is difficult to describe; it reminds me of screeching steel brakes on an enormous dump truck; a sound that starts on a low pitch and then soars high, is prolonged, and screeches to a stop. It is usually followed by a few guttural grunts or pants called "chuckles."

Listening to a bugling elk is a profound and privileged experience. It is unique to hear an age-old sound from the distant past, which holds the promise of the future. Bugling is indeed the vocal proclamation that these creatures of ancient ancestry are once again ready to insure their heritage.

A Deeper Perspective

Appreciating and experiencing the wonder of God in all of His creation has been the human experience since the very beginning of time:

> Ever since the creation of the world his eternal power and divine nature, invisible though they are, have been understood and seen through the things he has made. (NRSV Bible, Rom. 1.20)

Even if you've never read Romans 1, you are probably familiar with this well-known verse by Cecil Francis Alexander:

> All things bright and beautiful,
> All creatures great and small,

All things wild and wonderful,
The Lord God made them all.

Elk watching fills my senses, but it goes even deeper. The
sight and sound of these majestic creatures touches my soul
and inspires my spirit to a reverence of their Creator and mine.
I am awe-struck by the regal beauty of these majestic and
ancient creatures of the earth, and I am amazed by the continuing order of nature, the seasons, and life itself.

I like to think that the bugling of the elk at dawn and at
dusk, like the singing of birds in the morning and at sundown,
or the howling of the wolf at night, is a robust and echoing
song of praise. Such praise is vocal acknowledgment of the
greatness of the Creator by the creature simply doing what it
was created to do.

Belief in the Creator makes enormous sense to me. Only
the great God of the universe could hold all things in perfect
order. Creation affirms it again and again as we silently look and
listen.

Where are the Elk?

Jim Garvin, an experienced hunter in Rawlins, Wyoming,
once told me, "They're where you see 'em." I think I understand what he meant. Elk are wild animals and they don't stay
put. This is true for the Pennsylvania elk as well as the elk in
Wyoming. They roam around a lot in search of food, especially at first light and again at dusk. That is when they emerge
from the wooded forests to feed in the grassy openings and on
the food plots as well as on the lawns and bushes around the
local camps and houses. So that's where and when you'll see
'em…more or less.

I've learned from experience that when someone tells you
that wild animals are "where you see 'em," they usually have a
pretty good idea of where to look for them. Jim Garvin took me
to see a baby antelope and we ended up seeing a mother ante-

lope remove the sack from her newborn calf, just beyond a fairway on the golf course in Sinclair, Wyoming. We watched the calf stand for the first time and look at its mother, nose to nose, in a precious mother-child bonding moment that I will always remember. He also took me to a ranch and showed me two great horned owls that still had their downy feathers. The mother owl eyed us closely from a nearby tree. Jim is a hunter with a great love for wildlife. He knows the animals and what they do during the various seasons. That's why he can usually find them.

With the population of the Pennsylvania elk herd at an all-time high, it is relatively easy to see the elk during any season of the year. A large percentage of the herd occupies the area around the village of Benezette, which is why there is a very good chance you will see elk there. Often, elk may be found along Rt. 555 (the Pennsylvania Elk Highway) between Weedville and Driftwood, or anywhere along Winslow Hill Road. The Scenic Elk Viewing Area on State Game Land (SGL) 311 on Winslow Hill Road provides a panoramic view of open meadows near forest cover, edge conditions which elk find appealing.

For the more adventuresome, there are several gravel and dirt roads on the traditional elk range. These roads sometimes have ruts and washboard bumps, but if you have a truck or if your car needs realignment anyway, try these roads for variety: Gray Hill Road, Summerson Road, Dent's Run, and Hick's Run.

On the expanded range, but within a couple of miles of the traditional range, I like to watch for elk along the Quehanna Highway, going south from the Medix Run junction at Rt. 555. In the spring and summer of 2001, my husband Mike and I saw a group of bachelor bulls in velvet on several occasions, including a monster bull elk with an enormous 8 x 10 (eight by ten) rack of velvet-covered antlers which were not yet fully developed. In other words, he had 8 antler points on one side and 10 on the other! But, shhhh! Don't tell anybody!

Also, we enjoy driving down Rt. 120 from Emporium through Cameron, Sterling Run, Driftwood, and even to Sinnemahoning. Two of the largest bulls we saw in the summer of 2001 were in the village of Cameron feeding on a lawn at 7:11 a.m.!

Time of day is a critical element to consider when planning your elk watching trip. If you are in elk country within the first two or the last two hours of daylight when the elk are moving from the woods into the open areas to feed, your chances of seeing them are excellent. During the daytime, they frequently lie down in the shade of the woods and chew their cud. During the rut in autumn, elk move around more, and your chances of seeing elk and hearing bulls bugling are maximized.

On numerous visits to Benezette throughout various months and seasons, I've only missed seeing elk on one trip in 1995. I've seen between 20 and 50 elk on a typical road trip during any given month of the year, and I have seen and counted as many as 74 in a single trip.

As the herd continues to grow, elk watching opportunities in the expanded range areas will continue to increase as well. Between 1998 and 2000, 70 elk on the traditional range were trapped and transferred by the Pennsylvania Game Commission and released in the expanded elk range areas in western Clinton County, to the east of the traditional range (Cogan "Elk Hunt" 15). This was done to extend the population to the expanded elk range land and utilize its habitat, as well as to redistribute some of the concentrations of elk population and to help resolve conflicts with farmers and land owners in the traditional range areas. Some areas of the expanded elk range are more remote and have few public roads. Remote is good for elk, but not so good for elk watchers, especially those who like to do most of their scouting by car or truck.

Seasoned elk watchers may enjoy the challenge of searching for elk on the expanded range. But if you have limited time and want to be sure you will see elk in a single visit to elk country, your best bet is to look for them in and around the village of Benezette. Because the elk in this area are somewhat acclimated to being around people, you are likely to have the best chance for close elk sightings along with some great photo opportunities right along Rt. 555 and Winslow Hill Road. Some will even pose for pictures, leave autographs, and provide organic souvenirs! Be sure to check out the "elk droppings" jewelry in the local gift shops as well! I wonder if the elk have the items there on consignment to raise money to support their habitat. They are very resourceful animals, you know!

Elk Watchers' Code of Conduct

If you care about the elk and their future, you must do your best to demonstrate responsible behavior while visiting the elk range, for their protection and safety as well as your own.

In the excitement of sighting free-roaming elk at close range, visitors to elk country are also reminded to be safety conscious and considerate of the local residents as well as other visitors. Much of the 835 square mile range of the north central Pennsylvania elk herd is comprised of state game lands, state forest areas, and state parks. But nearly two -thirds of the 225 square miles of the traditional elk range is private property. The expanded elk range, on the other hand, which includes an additional 610 square miles, is comprised of approximately two-thirds public land and one-third private land (Kosack).

The following tips can keep you and the elk out of trouble during your visit.

Think: Safety First

- Never stop your vehicle in the road to watch or photograph elk. Be particularly careful on Rt. 555 where through traffic moves at a high rate of speed. When cars block the movement of one or both lanes of traffic on a public road, it creates a dangerous traffic hazard.
- Drive until you find a safe place to pull your car off of the road and onto the berm or shoulder of the road; then

walk cautiously along the side of the road back to where you saw the elk.

- Avoid parking your vehicle on a curve in the road.
- Do not feed the elk. An accidental brush of an antler can cause serious injury.
- Do not place your child in harm's way! Never place a child on or near an elk.
- During the rut, never stand between a bull and a cow, or between a bull and his harem. Sharp antlers, huge body size, raging hormones, and sharp hooves are four good reasons why.
- Do not stand between a cow and a calf. Cows are protective of their young and may swing a sharp hoof in your direction. At very least, they will look at you with disdain.
- Do not touch the elk. They are wild animals and may have ticks, scabies, or other parasites. The elk range is not a petting zoo.
- Observe tick precautions. North central Pennsylvania has a moderate to high risk of Lyme disease exposure, according to the Centers for Disease Control of the U.S. Public Health Service. The tiny black-legged deer ticks can carry Lyme disease. Ticks can attach themselves to skin and draw blood. They are usually acquired by walking through high grasses and brush. These are the recommended precautions:
  - Wear light–colored clothing, including a long-sleeved shirt and pants.
  - Tuck in shirts, and tuck pant legs into thick socks.
  - Wear smooth rather than furry fabrics.
  - Spray clothing with insect repellant.
  - Check clothing for ticks before re-entering your vehicle or home, especially after walking in high grass.

Be Respectful of the Elk –
You are a Guest on Their Home Range

- Leave pets at home. Besides being an annoyance to other visitors, noisy pets may be annoying to the elk, causing them to move back, and then you miss out on watching them. Pets on public land on the elk range must be kept on a leash at all times.
- Do not feed them. Feeding the elk from the back of a vehicle or from your hand acclimates the elk to expect food from humans. This gets the elk into a lot of trouble. Tempted as you may be to offer an apple to these magnificent beasts, keep in mind that if you do so, you are creating future problems for them. Approaching humans for food can be misinterpreted as aggression. Feeding elk along the roadways can also cause a traffic hazard, which can be dangerous for people as well as elk.
- Observe, but do not disturb. Keep a reasonable distance between the elk and you. If you approach a group of grazing elk and they begin to move away, you should back off. Allow the elk to be comfortable in your presence. Don't obstruct their path. Try not to interfere with their normal activities.
- Move slowly and quietly. Fast or sudden movements can be mistaken for aggression. Loud or unfamiliar noises are sometimes perceived as threatening.

Be Kind, Considerate, and Respectful of Residents
as Well as Other Tourists.

- Do not park on lawns or block driveways of local residents.
- Do not walk or drive on private property or posted land without permission.
- Avoid shining spotlights on houses or camps while spotting elk.

- Do not use elk calls late at night or early in the morning near camps and houses.
- Don't litter.
- Don't use offensive language. The elk don't like it.
- Be helpful and tolerant of others who may be visiting the elk range for the first time. Not everyone has learned how to be a responsible elk watcher. Converse with other visitors about the elk and share these tips if you have an opportunity.
- Become a role model of responsible elk watching behavior.

Things to Bring on Your Elk Watching Trip:

- Jacket and boots
- Blaze-orange vest in autumn
- Binoculars or spotting scope
- Camera; a zoom lens is a plus
- Moistened towelettes or handi-wipes (necessities for hand-washing after using the port-a-john)
- Carloads of courtesy, pounds of patience, and a good measure of common sense
- A note pad or journal and a pen to write down your elk watching experiences: record the date, time, location, and comments.

Things to Leave at Home:

- Pets
- Food for the elk (Remember that it is illegal to feed the elk.)
- Bad manners

Enjoy your visit to Elk Country! Maybe I'll see you there!

III

THE ELK WATCHER'S JOURNAL

This segment includes some of the elk watching experiences of the author, throughout the various months and seasons of the year. Interesting nuggets of knowledge about elk characteristics and behavior, including body weight and size, antlers, coat, feeding habits, reproduction, and elk communication are integrated into the elk watching descriptions. For a most enjoyable and educational visit to the Pennsylvania elk range, right from the comfort of your favorite easy chair, read on!

First Elk Watching Trips

May 1995: Carol's First Elk

On a mild and sunny Mother's Day afternoon, my husband Mike, my mother-in-law Frances, and I took a leisurely Sunday afternoon drive to the elk range. We came down from Emporium and through Driftwood. When we were in Benezette township traveling along PA Rt. 555, the "Elk Highway," we noticed a car that was pulled off on the side of the road. The people standing nearby were looking and pointing across the road. On the high side of the road, in the grassy yard of a house, a cow elk was lying down chewing her cud and enjoying the spring sunshine! Of course, she appeared larger than any deer I had ever seen, but it was difficult to evaluate her size since she wasn't standing up. I was amazed that she did not get up and run away, even when she knew people were watching her. But then, I thought, why should elk be intimidated at all? They are so much bigger than humans!

We saw other cows as we continued on our drive. Each was quite tall. I later learned that a cow elk weighs an average of 500 pounds, and stands 4 1/2 feet high *at the shoulder*. Add a long and sleek neck and it is roughly the size of a horse. The length from nose to tail averages 6 1/2 feet.

At first, the sight of their white rumps concerned me, and I wondered what terrible fate had befallen them that would have taken the fur off of their behinds and left them as white as a baby's bottom! Also, typical of the spring season, the elk were molting or shedding their heavy, grayish-white winter coats, and it was not a very pretty sight. I felt sorry for them. The word "beautiful" never came to mind. "Big"— yes — "huge" for that matter, but not beautiful. They looked scraggly to me.

Over the past few years, I've made numerous visits to the elk range and observed the elk in the various seasons and growth cycles. I've read about them and learned about some of their distinguishing characteristics and now I understand the changes in their appearance throughout the seasons. I've seen them at their best and at their worst, and I know their history. Somehow, in the process, I have grown to love the elk. When you grow to love someone or something, an incredible transformation of perception takes place. Now, every elk I see is absolutely beautiful! Although I must admit they look their worst in the spring, I love them, every one! In the spring, I call them "shabby chic!"

First Bull Elk on Winslow Hill

I recall the first bull elk I ever saw standing in the woods along the side of Winslow Hill Road when it was still a dirt road. He was browsing his way down a slope from the road, so I only got to see his wapiti (white rump) side. I wanted to get a better look at him, but he moved down the hill and out of sight all too soon. I don't remember how many points his antlers had, but I do remember that he was very large. At last I had seen a bull elk…at least from the wapiti side!

We drove up the hill, turned around, and were starting back down the dirt road. Across from where we had seen the first bull, three more bull elk were standing less than twenty feet away on a slope on the side of Winslow Hill Road near Summerson Road! A front and side view of these enormous creatures took my breath away! Maybe they looked so huge because they were standing on the upper slope of the hill, or maybe it was the thrill of seeing them so close. They were so tall that I had to tilt my head back to look up at them! They were taller than horses! Bull elk weigh an average of 700 pounds and a record bull can reach 1,100 pounds. On average, they stand five feet at the shoulder and are eight feet long from nose to tail. Getting a good look their awesome size as well as their antlers in velvet in May was very exciting and scary as well.

I was afraid to get out of the car to take a photograph! But I mustered the courage, leaving the car door open on the passenger side so I could make a quick retreat if necessary! My heart was beating out of my chest! I'm a lot smarter now. I make sure to close car doors and pull fully off of the road before getting out to take any photos. Seeing bull elk at close proximity is very exciting! But it's no excuse for ignoring common sense and safety practices.

June 1999: First Bulls in Yellowstone

Likewise, my first sighting of two bull elk with antlers covered in velvet in Yellowstone National Park in the summer of 1999 is etched in my memory. I'm glad it's etched somewhere, because it was a scene right out of a storybook, and, alas, my camera wasn't working! It was June and the coat or pelage of the elk was copper-colored and short, showing off their sleek musculature. They appeared very fit and well groomed. The antler spread of each bull elk had to be four feet wide! The morning mist had just lifted in a large grassy meadow along the road and they were a sight to behold — like something out of Camelot! They looked like giants compared to the white-tailed deer I was accustomed to seeing. They didn't seem to be deterred by the growing group of spectators nor by the intermittent flashes from several cameras. Some adults as well as children ran in rather close to get a better look. A Park Ranger tried to coax the crowd of about thirty spectators back to a twenty-yard distance. People were so excited to see such magnificent animals in the wild! I was exhilarated! Meanwhile, the elk quietly went about their business of grazing and looking awesome. They were still there when my husband Mike and I drove away about twenty minutes later.

An Increased Appreciation

Our trip to Yellowstone National Park and the Grand Teton National Park in Wyoming in the summer of 1999 was a trip to remember. It expanded my perspective and appreciation of wildlife and the importance of habitat land in America. I returned from our trip with a renewed appreciation of the elk we have right here in the beautiful forests of Pennsylvania, and a realization that our elk are second to none. My enthusiasm and interest in our elk herd rose to new heights, and haven't subsided since. I realized how blessed we are to have these huge, magnificent creatures inhabiting our forests. And I am happy and thankful to be living in rural Pennsylvania, just 65 miles north of the elk range!

Since the summer of 1999, I have made dozens of trips to the Pennsylvania elk range to observe and photograph the elk. I have purchased and read numerous books and articles about the elk in an effort to learn more about them, and I have researched various web sites for elk information. At this point, I must admit to being a certifiable "elkaholic!" Show me another elk!

Elk vs. White-Tailed Deer

It is difficult for me to understand how anyone could mistake an elk for a white-tailed deer. There is such an enormous difference in size, coloring, and antlers. First of all, elk are about five times larger than the average white-tailed deer. The only exception is that elk calves are almost the same size and color of some white-tailed deer during August and September. But during the deer-hunting season in November and December, there should be no mistaking an elk for a deer by anyone who has watched or studied the elk.

White-tailed deer have tails that are often between 12 and 15 inches long. On the dorsal side, their tails are brown and black, with white hair from the underside showing in stark contrast around the edges of the tail. They flip their tails up like a flag, showing the entirely white underside, when they turn to run away. Elk tails are short, only 4 to 5 inches in length, and sometimes look like a tuft of cotton on a large-bodied elk. Their tails don't flip and wave. Once you become familiar with the whitish or buff-colored rump patch of the wapiti and their very short white tails, elk are easily distinguishable from white-tailed deer.

Elk grow two very different coats each year – one in the spring and one in the fall. The spring coat is short and copper-colored, including the mane or neck hairs. The winter coat is grayish white with very dense, woolly hair underneath and coarse, long, hollow guard hairs on top, forming an insulating coat for protection from snow and moisture. In the fall, they grow long dark guard hairs on the neck as well, and so they look like they are wearing a whitish fur coat with a dark fur collar. The leg coloring remains dark brown, almost black, all year long. If you only ever saw elk in the fall, you might be quite surprised at how different they look in the summer.

How do elk antlers compare with white-tailed deer antlers? This is a "no-contest," a "no-brainer." The elk win, hooves down! …and antlers up! Deer antlers grow up and out and then most all points turn forward. Bull elk, on the other hand have much larger antlers with tines or points which resemble a giant pitchfork in the front at the brow line. In fact, these first two tines of the antlers on each side are named in order: the first, starting from the inside, is the "brow" tine, the second is the " bay" or "bez" tine (Murie 77). Mature elk antlers have a long main beam on each side, extending up, out, and back, with numerous tines or points extending from the main beam. Typical antlers for a mature bull elk have six points on each antler. The main beams can reach a length and span of 3 to 5 feet, and sometimes even 6 feet for a record bull.

April 8, 2001: Lightheaded Royalty

I had been waiting for some nice weather to take a spring trip to elk country. This was the day. It was sunny and 81 degrees, and I was reminding myself not to expect any great photo sessions since the bulls would be without their antlers, and the elk look very shabby in the spring before they shed their winter coats. Still, I was not expecting what I was about to see.

I made the usual loop of Winslow Hill and Rt. 555. I spotted a single elk grazing near one of the camps and pulled ahead to the side of the road to check it out. As expected, no antlers. But as I watched, he moved closer.

I talked to the bull elk and hummed softly as I often do when I'm alone, and he began to walk down the hill straight toward me, his posture regal and his head held high. Sure enough, the pedicles or bumps on his skull confirmed the fact that he was a bull who had shed his antlers recently. He had beautiful brown eyes and didn't seem to mind the fact that I was standing there watching him. As he came closer, I told him that I was just a little bit nervous since he was so much bigger than I was, and I stepped slowly to the left, toward my vehicle and took a picture of him as he crossed the road beside me. He told me that he'd been feeling lightheaded lately and asked me if I had seen his antlers anywhere! At least, that is what I *pictured* him saying! I watched as he wandered across the road and into the back yard of a nearby camp, pausing to nibble a few leaves along the way.

Keeping Antlers in April

After awhile I turned and looked back across the road to the slope from which the antlerless bull had descended. Lo and behold, there came another bull, but this one still had antlers! This 4-point followed the same path and routine as the other bull. He paused and grazed, checked me out, decided to come straight down anyway, and I moved out of the way again, and snapped a photo of him crossing the road. I pictured this one saying, " I've decided to keep my antlers...I hear they are worth money!" I smiled, dreaming of how nice it would be if he'd shed them in the road right then and there!

I had read that bulls usually don't shed both antlers at the same time. Getting a set of sheds that easily would be a rare miracle. But it actually happened for Larry Jones, the "Elk Whisperer" and author who lives in Idaho. A bull elk he had befriended during a hard winter shed both of his antlers right in Larry's driveway, side by side (Jones 171). But it didn't happen for me on that April day in Pennsylvania. Maybe someday...and when it does, I'll know it's a gift.

The antlered bull crossed the road and joined the other near a woodpile behind a camp. Two people were sitting in the yard near a campfire. The bulls seemed undeterred by their presence. After leisurely browsing on the budding bushes, they wandered further back into the woods.

I hopped into my SUV and drove back down Winslow Hill, still amazed at having seen a bull with antlers in April. It must be a fluke, I thought. There were cars stopped beside a field near Youngmark Road. In the field was a group of cows and yearlings, a small spike bull that still had his antlers, and another bull with skimpy branched antlers. It wasn't such a fluke after all!

Return to Royal Splendor

As I reached the bottom of Winslow Hill, I saw something else I hadn't expected. There on the green lawn across the road behind the Benezette Hotel were three bulls with thick velvet-covered knobs growing on their heads! They looked like fist-sized protrusions from which thick finger-like extensions sprouted. The bulls were lined up side by side, feeding in unison. And of course, it was twilight and the few pictures I took showed only dark shadows with glowing eyes.

But seeing these bulls was exciting because it made me realize that these elk were already making their return to royal splendor by donning their new velvet headgear. It was a promise of things to come. I later concluded that these were probably mature bulls which had most likely shed their antlers in February or March, and were off to a good start on growing new ones in April!

All totaled, I saw 24 elk on that Palm Sunday afternoon. I hadn't expected to see any antlers in April, and instead I saw old antlers, new velvet-covered antlers, and pedicles ready to start growing antlers. It was all quite amazing to me.

Antler Shedding

A few months later, I was reading the book, *The Elk of North America* by Olaus Murie. A field naturalist in the early twentieth century, he was recognized worldwide as the foremost authority on elk and caribou in North America. His book, originally published in 1951 by Knopf, is considered by many to be the most comprehensive work ever done on the elk. Murie's detailed and specific observation-based writing provides very interesting and useful information for elk watchers.

For 36 years, Murie studied the elk in the Jackson Hole area in Wyoming. I really enjoy reading his book because he often wrote about variations and gave so many examples. He said that March is the month in which most bulls will shed their antlers. However, he also gave examples of older and mature bulls dropping their antlers in February, and some two-year old bulls holding their antlers as late as May, and spike bulls having the widest variation in shedding dates, some as early as February and as late as June (Murie 81). He made it clear that there were wide variations in his observations. Reading his book helped me make sense of the different stages of elk antler shedding and development that I was seeing in April.

Antlers of Young Bull Elk

According to Murie's writings, certain antler characteristics can give clues to the age of a young bull. For instance, a spike bull, or a one-year-old usually grows a single thin antler on each side, varying from 10 to 20 inches long (77). Sometimes the spike may have a fork on the tips of the antlers or some thin tines branching off of the antlers. After his second birthday, the bull will usually grow antlers with tines branching off of a main beam that sweeps back. The antlers of a two-year-old bull usually have 4 to 5 points on each side, sometimes fewer than 4 or as many as 6 points, but the antlers are still rather slender and small compared to those of a mature bull elk. The antler spread or distance between the tips of each beam is also less than the 3 to 5 feet spread which is characteristic of mature bull antlers. Young bulls with slender and spindly antlers are sometimes referred to as "raghorns." Murie also noted that in younger bulls, the pedicles (place of attachment of the antlers to the skull) are elongated (81). As antlers are grown and lost each successive year, the resorbsion of some of the bone at the pedicle is thought to be the reason for the shortening and thickening of the pedicle as the bull matures (qtd in Murie 81). The antlers of a three-year-old are distinguished from the two-year-old only in the thickness of the antler and in the pedicle, which is thicker and shorter (Murie 80). In *Among the Elk*, author David Petersen further explains that with each successive growth year, the pedicles lengthen on the inner surfaces, while shortening on the outer edges (41). Thus the angle between the antlers becomes widened, resulting in a wider antler spread or distance between the beam tips with each successive growth and shedding sequence (Petersen 41).

The second bull I saw on that April day was a 4 x 5 point with raised or elongated pedicles and slender antlers, which spanned between 2 and 3 feet, and were probably no more than 3 feet long. These characteristics are typical of a bull between two and three years of age. From this I deducted that the bull I saw that was still holding his second set of antlers in April was almost three years old.

Elk Teeth

Although number of points and the thickness of the antlers are an indication of elk maturity, it is not an exact indicator of the age of the bull, as some people believe. Teeth are the most accurate indicators of the age of an elk. By looking at a cross section of an elk's tooth, biologists can determine the age by the number of growth rings. Of course, this is not something the average elk watcher will be doing!

Elk teeth can sometimes be seen when a bull raises his

head and curls his upper lip to display his dominance or to bugle, or just before he is ready to charge. If you see an elk's teeth bared, you'd better get out of his way!

The upper canine teeth of the elk are noteworthy because they are actually small tusks made of ivory. Long ago, Native Americans and mountain men would decorate their clothing with elk ivories. They were a treasured possession in many western tribes. As recently as the early part of the twentieth century, elk were sometimes killed by poachers motivated by greed, solely for their two upper canine teeth which were sold and fashioned into fine jewelry. As recently as the early 1900's, more than 500 elk were poached in Yellowstone National Park for their canine teeth and their carcasses were left to rot. The elk ivories were purchased and used as membership tokens by a fraternal organization named for the elk (Krakel 89). What a sad irony!

April 22, 2001: Return to Winslow Hill

It was two weeks later when Mike and I returned to the elk range, hoping to again see the bulls with velvet antlers which would be growing bigger by now. I had hoped to see an obviously pregnant cow, but had read that they don't look much different except for maybe the last two weeks when the calf is carried low in the birth canal.

So we took the loop of Winslow Hill and Rt. 555, and as we rode along, I told Mike, for the second or third time, the detailed stories of the elk I has seen two weeks before, pointing out the precise areas where I had seen them.

Weakened Yearlings

In a grassy field just above Youngmark Road, we came upon a group of 46 cows, yearlings and a couple of bulls that had shed their antlers. This was a nice place to watch elk, with the wide berm on the right side of the road for safe parking.

I was somewhat startled to see a couple of very thin and scraggly-looking calves in this group. They were lying down part of the time, and when the one put his head flat to the ground, he looked ill. From all I had read about the elk, spring is a vulnerable time for the yearling calves, which are exhausted from the long hard winter. A late winter storm can sometimes be the last straw. But if they have made it this far and still have the strength to graze, they will begin the recovery, shed their winter coats, and start to thrive once again. Still it alarmed my heart to see the young ones looking so puny and exhausted. So I did the single thing I could do: I prayed for their survival.

Bull Elk Crossing the Bennett's Branch

When we drove back down to the Benezette Store, one of our usual stops, I noticed some folks looking with binoculars in the direction of the Bennett's Branch of Sinnemahoning Creek behind the store. They were watching a bull in velvet crossing the stream! Man, oh, man! If I could only get a picture of that! By the time I got close enough to snap a picture, the bull had reached the bank, and proceeded to shake the water off of his heavy, tattered, grayish-white winter coat in what looked like slow motion. Then, for the next twenty minutes or so, he fed on new spring leaves sprouting on the bushes and grazed on the green sedges growing along the bank of the Bennett's Branch behind the store.

Talks With Elk

Meanwhile, two cow elk proceeded to cross the river further down and I could see their distant silhouettes against the sunset as they moved across the water. But I decided not to leave the bull to attempt to get the other photo. I continued to watch him browse amongst the bushes along the bank of the river branch. He was visible from the road near the bridge and I was able to get some awesome photos using a simple zoom lens. I was talking to him softly as usual, and telling him how beautiful he was. As I stood in a clear area to get a photo, he looked straight at me, then slowly pulled his head back and I could see the cleft in his upper lip. He brought his head back down, looked at me again and calmly repeated the communication. I knew without a doubt what he was saying: "Move back; I'm coming through." Without hesitation I stepped to the side of the opening and quietly walked back up the road to the front of the restaurant.

Coming through is exactly what he had in mind. He walked right through the place where I had been standing to photograph him! Mike watched as he came up to the asphalt drive, then climbed the steep grassy slope up to Rt. 555. When he got to the top, he paused, looked both ways as if watching for traffic, before crossing the road to graze on the greening lawns on the other side.

I think if I had a Native American name, it would not be *Dances With Wolves*, but it would probably be *Talks With Elk*, *Dances with Chippies*, or *Sings With Squirrels*! Take your pick. I've done all three! Mostly, I talk with elk. This bull in velvet communicated with me by using body language and I understood exactly what he was saying. Dominance posturing is a common means of communication among elk. If you watch them enough, you begin to understand what they mean by their sounds and body language. I will gladly yield the right of way to them anytime. After all, it's their home territory, and they have places to go and fields to graze. I'm just there for recreation. And besides, they are a lot bigger than I am!

The Elk Lick

As we drove back along Rt. 555 between Benezette and Medix Run, there were numerous cars parked along the road near a place called "General Potter's: The Big Elk Lick." Mike and I often see elk on this property, along with horses and campers. This night was no exception. It is a place we seldom stop, however. Curves in the road, fast moving traffic and the narrow berm along Rt. 555 make it hazardous to park in this area without blocking someone's driveway.

Nevertheless, I do have a fond memory of General Potter's place. One night as Mike and I were leaving the elk range and driving past General Potter's, there were two large bull elk right along the road! We had our neighbor Joyce Powell and Mike's mom with us that evening and they enjoyed seeing a couple of bull elk up close without having to get out of the vehicle. It was a highlight of their trip!

Speaking of elk licks, particularly in early spring, elk seek the minerals contained in both natural and artificial elk licks to replenish diminished stores. Magnesium, inorganic sulfur, and sodium help with the digestive process and protein synthesis (Geist 141). Calcium is needed for the bulls to grow strong bones and antlers, for pregnant cows to produce strong calves, and for lactating cows to produce milk. The elk require minerals to grow new coats as well. Although they eat leaves such as aspen and other plants that are high in calcium, it is common to see elk at mineral licks on the elk range during the springtime. They seem to be drawn to the sites. I think elk licks are to elk what baking soda biscuits are to people; every now and then you get a craving for them that nothing else will satisfy. They do settle the stomach and satisfy a craving.

May 6, 2001 Sunday: Heaven's Meadow

It was a 78 degree summer-like evening on Winslow Hill and we were turning around to head back to town. Then a truck of elk watchers stopped and a guy got out to tell us that there was a group of 40 elk in a meadow just a short distance ahead. So, what the heck, we decided to check it out.

We parked off of the road and walked along the path toward the grassy meadow. It was the first time I had walked out onto the game lands in this particular area to see the elk. Three other folks with cameras were just leaving. They had counted 42 elk. As Mike and I approached the area slowly and quietly, I had an overwhelming sense of the peacefulness of this secluded place; it was heavenly! Suddenly we were immersed in the world of the elk.

All I could hear was an occasional songbird singing its evening solo, the slight creaking of a dead tree limb swaying in the soft breeze, and the faint crackling sound of a chipmunk or field mouse moving through the dried leaves and brush. Occasionally a soft mew or chirp could be heard from a cow or yearling.

There in the grassy knoll which unfolded before us, was a group of cows and yearlings grazing peacefully. The matriarch cow as well as other sentinel cows on lookout duty spotted us and gave us a few stares. We stopped and decided to keep our distance. When I moved around to snap a few photos and moved back, one of the cows barked a warning alarm. Others then lifted their heads to look and listen to determine if in fact there was a threat. Then the group resumed grazing undisturbed, which pleased me. If the elk had felt threatened, they would have begun to move away.

I'm getting much better at not disturbing the elk, realizing how important it is to avoid stressing them or causing them to waste their energy, particularly at this vulnerable time of the year. The yearling calves, still thin and shabby looking from the long winter, needed to feed undisturbed to regain their strength and grow their summer coats. Likewise, the pregnant cows, which would deliver their calves within the next 4 to 6 weeks, needed the nutritional boost of the succulent spring grasses and plants to help them produce healthy, sizable offspring.

Sometimes, rather than photographing them, I find it is more enjoyable just watching the elk and basking in the ambiance of the moment. The thing I will remember most about this elk sighting is the absolute peacefulness of this group of cows and yearlings grazing in the lush green meadow nestled between the woods on State Game Land 311. This is their home, and I realized what a privilege it was to witness such a scene in the life of the Pennsylvania elk. Not everyone in the world has this priceless opportunity.

A Yearling Running Sprints

On our way back, we spotted a couple of cows and yearlings near the stream along Rt. 555. One of the yearlings started prancing then galloping along the railroad grade parallel to the water. He stopped on a dime, then ran back, stopped again, and repeated the routine! His mother didn't appear particularly impressed by his sprints and continued walking with the other cows toward the stream. We, on the other hand, were cheering the young sprinter on as we watched from our vehicle, enjoying the candid display of a yearling at play! It was quite a show. It proved yet again that you never know just what surprising things you might see when you go elk watching.

Thursday, May 10, 2001: The Deal

Here was the deal: It was 74 degrees and mostly sunny and Mike was going to St. Marys to watch a high school baseball game where Bradford High was playing. If I wanted to go to the game, we could then go on to Benezette to see the elk. OK, it's a deal! We cheered for our friends' son Shane and it was an exciting game, which the Bradford team ended up winning 6-4. Then off we headed to elk country. Yahoo!

Back to the Peaceful Meadow

We went back to the meadow where we had seen the group of cows and yearlings three days before. I counted 24. Four were lying down chewing their cud and appeared very relaxed. This time, although we got a few looks from the cows and a single snort, there was no bark of alarm. We're getting better all the time at not disturbing them.

Cud Chewing

Elk have a four-chambered stomach, which is very handy for processing large quantities of food of various textures. They consume grass and plants quickly and store the undigested food in the first chamber. Then they will lie down and bring a bolus or ball of the food mixture back up into their mouths and chew it again, or "ruminate." The bolus of food is called "cud." When the thoroughly chewed cud is swallowed, it passes on into the next chamber. The process of digestion is continued in the additional chambers where fermentation and bacterial breakdown of the food takes place.

Knuckle Popping

Sometimes while quietly observing a group of elk, you can hear a sound that is similar to knuckles popping. It is a noise made by the legs of the elk as they walk around. This noise serves as a method of communication, since it indicates the approach or movement of other elk nearby. When they are moving through the woods, the elk can keep track of the location of other elk by those familiar sounds.

Just One More Drink

One small yearling tried to nurse and with the upward poke of his head, nudged his mother's back feet off of the ground! He was just too big for that routine, and her milk had probably dried up many months ago. Perhaps he remembered his nursing days of last summer. Maybe he was having a hard time adjusting to the new diet of spring grasses; or maybe he was just plain thirsty! Who knows? In any case, his behavior was "udderly" surprising to me!

The cow had a yellow radio collar, and I couldn't help but wonder if it was the same mother and calf that I had photographed the previous autumn. I had wondered how that young calf, apparently born late in the season, would fare through the winter, since it was somewhat small and still nursing in late October. If this was the same calf, it hadn't changed much in size, but it did survive the winter! That is a very major accomplishment for a small elk calf.

Lazy Grazing Through the Woods

We heard the snaps and cracks of breaking twigs, with the movement of two more cows in the woods to our right. They stopped to check us out, and then resumed grazing, moving parallel through the woods along the side of the meadow. The floor of the forest is rich with new green growth in the springtime and the elk love to graze on the tender plants, which are not available to them through the winter. We waited for them to emerge into the clearing but they were very intent on grazing along the path through the woods. Finally, we decided to move on in search of some velvet-antlered bulls.

Looking for Velvet

By springtime, the bulls have teamed up into bachelor groups in search of food in areas separate from the cows and yearling calves. As the days become longer, the length of daylight or the "photo-period" stimulates the hypothalamus, which signals the production of testosterone in the elk. The testos-

terone stimulates the regrowth of antlers. It is the beginning of the hormonal cycle of the bull, which culminates with the rut in autumn (Furtman 98). During this time, nutritional needs are increased as the velvet antlers grow as much as an inch per day, and the better the nutrition, the healthier the bull, and the bigger the antlers. Of course, age of the bull and genetics have a major effect on the size and configuration of the antlers, but nutritious habitat gives the bull a great advantage.

Elk on the Playground

We made a quick check behind the Benezette Store, where we had watched a bull in velvet cross the stream a few weeks before, but no elk were in sight. Sigh! We decided to head back home. As we pulled out on to Rt. 555 at dusk, I was wondering where the bulls might be, and then I spotted a bull in velvet grazing in the playground of the red brick schoolhouse! We pulled off in front of the school and watched him for awhile. I noticed his winter coat was almost completely shed and he was sporting his new copper-colored summer coat. His antlers were beige-colored and fuzzy, and already appeared to be about 15 inches long. The forked rounded ends on the tips of the main beams reminded me of dog bones! He was in great shape compared to the cows and yearlings we had seen earlier. We enjoyed taking a few photos of him in the quickly fading daylight.

A Monster Bull in the Making

A man and woman pulled up in a truck beside us and told us that they had seen an even bigger bull behind the school. We didn't have to move far to find him. He was grazing and browsing his way along the side of the brick building toward the swing set in the playground, moving in our direction. We watched him graze his way along past the sliding board and the seesaws, and around the colorful plastic animal figures on the playground. It was both amusing and amazing.

I had returned to my vehicle to watch him. Twilight precluded any great picture taking at this point, but as this bull grazed closer and closer to where we were parked, he was really a sight to behold! His body was much larger than the other bull we had photographed, and his head and neck were gigantic. His velvet antlers already spanned at least 30 inches and appeared perfectly symmetrical. He was already a 4-point bull (which means four antler points on each side) and the main beam of each antler looked like a fat baseball bat jutting out of his skull on each side. From this beam would stem even more antler points over the next few months.

It makes my heart race when a bull gets so close that I can look into his big brown eyes. I always feel safer remaining in the vehicle and letting the bull wander near if he wants to. And that is exactly what happened. He came to within ten feet of our SUV. I nervously snapped a couple of photos, knowing it was too dim. This was no ordinary bull. I couldn't believe the size of the pedicles from which his velvet antlers had sprouted!

Scrounging for Food in April

"It's Been a Long Winter!"

"I'm Keeping My Antlers!"

"I'm Growing New Ones!"

Country Girl

"My Mother Says I'm Getting Taller"

Mother-To-Be

Nursing Calf

"Pick Your Ride!"

"Slugger's My Name; Baseball's My Game!"

Pretty Cowgirl

"You Can Call Me Bud."

Bull Elk in Cameron

Kindergarten

Synchronized Grazing

Big, Lean, Grass-Eating Machine

"These Antlers Bend Like Rubber!"

Live Lawn Art

Big and Bigger

Hanging Out at Camp

Polishing Antlers in August

Cruising for Elk Chicks

Harem Recruitment

A Perfect "Six"

Majestic Bull Elk

Little Mus-Koose

Monarch of the Meadow

Small Harem

Bull in Camouflage

Bugle Boy

Swing Set Fetish

Woolly Bully

His pedicles were easily 3 1/2 inches in diameter, with no exaggeration – the size of the opening in a white Styrofoam coffee cup with a circumference of 9 1/2 inches! They were the largest I had ever seen. Wow! What a dandy! As I watched him, I imagined that in past autumns he was undoubtedly an experienced harem master, who would again be a major contender in the autumn rut. Even this early in the season, I would not hesitate to nominate him as the big bull of the year! This bull has great potential! What an impressive animal! On that Thursday evening at 8:09 p.m., no one was there watching him except Mike and me. Once again, I felt privileged to witness such a sight. I'll remember the size of those pedicles for a long time to come, and hope I get to see this bull again sometime.

Bachelor Party of Five in Caledonia

If that wasn't enough excitement for one evening, there was one more treat in store. As we made the turn up the Old Caledonia Road heading toward St. Marys, I spotted a bull in velvet on the back lawn of a house along Rt. 555. We turned around and went back to check it out. There was a bachelor party of five, with velvet antlers in various stages of growth, grazing in the yard. This was a treat because it was the first time we had seen elk in Caledonia on our many trips to Benezette. So now I had at least a partial answer to my question, "Where are the bachelor bulls?" These five were having dinner in Caledonia.

Baseball, Elk, and Burgers

Watching elk eat for an hour and a half made us hungry. All totaled, we saw 45 elk on this trip. Our last stop on the way home was the Wendy's in St. Marys for a couple of bacon cheeseburgers. Somehow, food always tastes better after spending time outdoors in the fresh air. Why is that?

June 7, 2001: Visitors from Wyoming

On June 7th, 2001, Mike's cousin Sharon and her friend Steve were in Pennsylvania for a visit. Both of them are experienced big game hunters and enjoy wildlife as much as Mike and I do. I had promised to show them the elk in Pennsylvania. So the four of us were off to elk country in my "rig," as Wyoming folks would say. Both Mike and Steve brought good binoculars along on this trip. Steve works for the Wyoming Game and Fish Department and is a hunt guide as well. He really gets excited about elk! We made our usual stop at the Scenic Elk Viewing Area on Winslow Hill and Steve proceeded to find elk with his binoculars three hillsides away! In Wyoming, they are accustomed to searching for them on far away ridges. Sharon, who had shot a 5-point elk (5 x 5) three years ago, was very good at picking out elk on the far hillsides that Mike and I would have missed. I could hardly wait until they got a look at our elk at 20 or 30 feet!

We drove and walked out to a food plot on State Game Land 311, the place I call Heaven's Meadow, which was busy with cows and yearlings grazing on the flowering clover and other forbs and grasses. Usually an older cow or is the leader and chief sentinel of the group, who will signal the others of any approaching danger or threat. As we approached, the matriarch cow looked up. Steve told me to stop walking whenever she picked her head up and to take three more steps when she began feeding again. So I did that four times and was in great position for some photos with my zoom lens. The group remained undisturbed in our presence.

Sweet Clover in Heaven's Meadow

The lush green meadow was blanketed with vast stretches of fragrant white clover blossoms. On that sunny and balmy afternoon with the temperatures in the 80's, the sweet fresh scent of the clover was a new and unexpected treat to savor. Several bumblebees hummed in agreement as they buzzed from flower to flower enjoying the sweet treat. The cows and yearlings feeding peacefully and looking very healthy in their copper-colored summer coats confirmed the prevailing opinion that this meadow in the heart of the Pennsylvania elk range was indeed a little bit of heaven.

I'll never forget the sweet aroma of the blossoming clover in that tranquil elk meadow. Once again, I felt privileged, prayerful, and thankful for the beauty of nature and life itself. Someday, when I'm feeling stressed, I'll remember that heavenly meadow, and rekindle the attitude of prayer and gratitude which always brings an inner peace.

Matriarch Cows

Matriarchs, or experienced cows which have given birth to several generations of calves, lead the herds to familiar feeding grounds and to protective cover in winter, spring, and summer. They also serve as the guardians and protectors of the herd, barking calls of alarm and investigating any perceived threats. I had always figured that the big bulls were in charge! I learned that that is only true of harems of cows and calves during the rut. And it's no secret that during the rut, the cows pick the bulls and not the other way around! Even in the world of the elk, the females rule! They also do most of the work in raising their young and teaching them survival skills.

Bulls on Their Own

In the spring and summer, the bulls travel in small bachelor groups or forage alone. Once they have lost their antlers in late winter or early spring, they lose their hierarchy or place of rank in the herd, and go off to feed on their own. The bulls tend to roam more extensively than the mixed groups of cows and yearlings. Their nutritional demands are increased as their antlers grow as much as an inch per day. Besides grasses which provide protein, they need foliage and forbs rich in calcium, phosphates, and protein to support the growth of large antlers (Geist 57). It takes about the same amount of nutrition for a bull to grow a large rack of antlers as it does for a cow elk to grow a calf.

The bulls feed almost constantly during the summer. On a moonlit night, they'll continue feeding through most of the night. They are also increasing body mass in preparation for the massive energy expenditure of the rut, which will begin in September. It's all about breeding and it takes several months of preparation.

Expectant Cows

On this trip we did see a couple of obviously pregnant cows. One mother-to-be was eagerly feeding to produce a large calf with a better chance of survival. Steve said she would probably "drop her calf" (give birth) within the next two weeks. The only time the cow elk look heavy with their calves is during the two weeks before parturition or birthing, when the calf is carried low in the birth canal.

We drove back down Winslow Hill, and on the way, there was another group of 12 elk near Youngmark Road. One very pregnant cow was lying down. She looked like she was ready to go into labor any minute. Her underbelly was bulging with the calf. I excitedly thought of the prospect of seeing a new calf on my next visit to the elk range!

Big Bulls in Medix Run

When we got back to town, we decided to take a ride to Medix Run and out the Quehanna Road to the south. That was where we spied a group of bulls. There were five with antlers in velvet, in a field of tall grass on the left-hand side of the road. One was nestled down beside a pile of wood and brush and his antlers were very well camouflaged. Steve spotted it first. We had a lot of fun using the binoculars to check out these bulls. Even Steve was impressed by their size, and enjoyed watching them at relatively close range.

After about twenty minutes, we headed further south and saw a car pulled off on the right. A couple of folks were watching a monster bull browsing his way along through the woods. He was an 8 x 9 with huge antlers. We got out of the car and walked along the roadside to get a better look. This bull really was impressive. He had an antler that curled down in front of his right ear like a hook, and another that curled behind the ear as well. We estimated that the main beams on his antlers were already out four feet. This bull was a dandy and his antlers were not finished growing! In the fading light and the tree cover, there were no good photo opportunities to be had. But this was an elk we would remember. Since we had been within twenty feet of him, it was an "up-close-and-personal" experience, the kind that makes your heart race, takes your breath away, and makes you eager to come back again. I think that if I saw that bull again I would recognize him by the unusual antler configuration. Steve said he'd like to come back again to hunt elk in Pennsylvania.

I had come through on my promise of showing Steve and Sharon some Pennsylvania elk. All totaled, we saw 74 that day, and it was a wonderful and memorable elk watching experience for our Wyoming visitors. They also enjoyed the many trees along all the roadsides in Pennsylvania. It is a notable contrast to the Wyoming landscape, which is mostly wide open with high plains and deserts, and mountains in the distance, and with trees located primarily in the mountain forests.

Pregnant Cows and Parturition

In the days and weeks that followed, I thought about the pregnant cows and prayed for good weather for them. Many of the cows have been pregnant since late September or early October. The gestation period is 8 1/2 months, which means most calves will be born in late May or early June.

The cows go off alone, away from the herd, to give birth to their calves. Usually a cow will give birth to a single calf, but on rare occasions, twins are born. Calves are kept hidden for about two weeks, until they are large enough and strong enough to rejoin the herd. A newborn elk calf weighs an average of 30 to 35 pounds, stands within minutes, nurses within an hour, and runs fast within a week. The mother elk cleans the calf thoroughly by licking it several times a day, to remove any scent of urine, feces, or mother's milk, so that no predators will find her calf. The newborn quickly learns to drop to the ground and stay hidden among ferns and other plants at the mother elk's command. During the first few hours of life, the calf and the cow become imprinted with each other's scent and a strong bonding process begins. Often the cow will go off for hours at a time to graze and build her milk supply, and will return only periodically to feed her calf. A lactating cow will usually stay within one-quarter to one-half mile of a stream or other continuous water supply.

Elk Commotion

After about two weeks, the mother and calf will rejoin other cows, calves, and yearlings. Getting back into the herd is important for safety and protection from predators. There are many more eyes on the lookout, and elk communicate with each other and with their calves with certain sounds, like chirps, mews, and barks. Elk are among the noisiest of the ungulates or hoofed animals. Communication is important for identification between calves and cows, as well as to warn of potential threats. The calves learn quickly to obey the vocal commands of the mother elk. A visit to the elk range on an early summer morning can give you a true appreciation of "elk talk" as well as an interesting exposure to elk activity. There is plenty of commotion with calves and yearlings running, playing, and feeding intermittently.

Predators

In Pennsylvania, the elk do not have as many predators as the elk out West. Black bears, bobcats, and coyotes are among the predators of elk calves in Pennsylvania. In the West, wolves, grizzly bears, and mountain lions are added to the list of predators of elk. Calves are the most vulnerable.

June 13, 2001: A Lone Cow Chases Away a Yearling

On that sunny summer afternoon, I was really hoping to see some cows and calves. For the heck of it, I drove up the hill and walked out to Heaven's Meadow. This is the spot where we had seen a very pregnant cow elk two weeks earlier. Much to my surprise, there was a lone cow feeding in the blossoming clover! Hmm. Could she possibly have a calf nearby? She very likely did, because a few minutes later when a yearling spike, probably her offspring from the previous year, arrived on the scene, she shooed him away…twice…and then looked over into the grass to the right side of the meadow. Then she distracted him by decoying herself and running straight in the opposite direction, and the yearling followed her! They both disappeared into the timber. I was tempted to check the grassy area on the right side of the meadow, but I sure couldn't deal with a cow elk charging back across the meadow at me, in defense of her calf! I realized then that I was too timid to traipse across that meadow alone to look for a baby elk curled up in the tall grass, that day or any other day!

The Cow Song

Suddenly I was startled by a sound that resembled the bugling of a bull elk but was not nearly as loud or as strong. I had read that cows sometimes bugle in the spring and particularly during the calving season in May and June ("Calf Survival"). There was no one else around so I knew it was not an artificial call. I wondered if the cow that disappeared into the woods delivered that bugling sound as a bluff to any potential predators that a bull elk was nearby! I speculated that perhaps the cow elk bugle was a hormonal song. Whatever the cause, I was pleased to have heard it, particularly after having read about it.

In his book, *Season of the Elk*, Dean Krakel II says that a cow's bugling announces spring. He describes it as "part scream and wail, part whistle and howl," and goes on to say, "…the cow's heralding of spring is born of the stirrings of life within her own body and her exuberance at being released from winter's long, frigid confinement (110)." Then, indeed, the cow's bugle is a song of praise!

Bulls in the Ball Field

It never fails. As soon as I buy a frozen ice pop at the Benezette Store and it starts dripping, I see an elk! This time I had driven down to check for elk behind the red schoolhouse. There were three bulls in and near the old ball field in the back of the schoolyard! The fence on the back side did not deter two of the bulls from entering from the far side to eat the lush green grass there, which was now growing quite tall. The third bull remained outside of the fenced area.

The one bull had grown enormous antlers that reminded me of baseball bats. His antlers went "back, back, back!" He sported a growing 8 x 9 rack and was grazing vociferously. I slurped down my melting cherry ice pop and took the lens cap off of my camera. There was still plenty of daylight for photography! But when a bull is feeding continually, it is difficult to get a photo with his head in an upright position. I finally figured out how to do it. Whenever people approached, the bull would lift his head from grazing to check out their movement. This provided a five to seven second window of opportunity for an upright headshot! There were three other families of elk watchers that arrived while I was there that evening, including some campers from the Pittsburgh area. Everyone was quiet and well behaved and all were fascinated at the size of the bull in the ball field. Consequently, we enjoyed watching that bull for a long while, and had plenty of good photo opportunities. The two smaller bulls grazed nearby and then moved away.

As twilight fell, I moved out as well, and figured I could make it back to St. Marys before dark. Mike always reminds me, "Your vehicle has headlights – at least it did the last time I checked." That's true, but I still like to get out of elk country before the white-tailed deer start popping out in front of those headlights!

June 25, 2001: Flora and "Fawna"

The summer season is never complete without enjoying the antics of the white-tailed fawns on the elk range. While I was driving along Rt. 555 toward Grant, a doe with twin fawns crossed the road in front of me. White-tailed deer are skittish, and don't hang around long for picture taking. But in the springtime, they are very interesting to watch. I pulled off of the road and attempted a photo. The fawns frolicked in the woods, running, stopping, and curiously eyeing me. The doe led them away with dispatch, but not before I was able to get a quick photo.

I paused to look at the lovely orange daylilies blooming along the side of the road, and breathed a prayer of appreciation for both the flora and the fauna of elk country on that beautiful lazy summer afternoon.

Cowgirls

In my elk search that day, I did see a small group of five cows feeding in a grassy meadow at the bottom of Dewey Road. They looked very sleek and healthy, with their short, shiny, copper-colored pelage showing off their well-defined lean musculature. They were radiant, feeding on wildflowers in the blossoming meadow. One had a daisy in her mouth and reminded me of a Spanish dancer holding a rose stem between her teeth. I figured that these could be two-year old females, generally too young to give birth this spring, but they would probably have their first estrus or fertile period in September. Although it is possible for cow elk to breed at 16 months of age, most will breed for the first time when they are 28 months old. During the spring calving season the young cows are temporarily abandoned by the pregnant mother cows, which have gone off separately to give birth and to keep their new calves in hiding for two weeks. These "cowgirls" seemed content to be feeding together in the flowering meadow.

Cow Crossing the Bennett's Branch

Back along Rt. 555 near Hicks Run Road, I pulled off along the side of the road near Bennett's Branch of the Sinnemahoning Creek. There was a cow elk crossing the stream and I managed to get a photo! It wasn't as close as I would have liked, but it was a splendid treat to see her cross. I tried to position myself further down the road to see where she would come out, but the late June foliage was too dense to allow a good view.

Bachelor Group in Medix Run

I drove down to Medix Run and out the Quehanna Road a short distance, and spotted three bull elk feeding on grasses and flowering forbs near the right side of the road. Their antlers were getting huge now. I looked at them with Mike's good binoculars (the ones I have promised not to lose) and recognized the largest as being the monster bull that Steve and Sharon had admired! His bez tine on the right curved like a hook near his right ear. He also had a small tine that curled down behind his right ear, and another short tine that appeared to jut out sideways over his left ear. He was now clearly an 8 x 10 point with forks at the tips of at least three antler branches! His antlers weren't finished growing yet. The other two bulls with him were good-sized animals as well. All three were doing some serious grazing and foraging and seemed oblivious to my presence. After taking as many photos as I wanted, I turned back down the road toward Rt. 555. I later e-mailed Sharon and Steve the photos of the big bull elk they had admired.

Antlers that have an unusual configuration may indicate an injury or damage during the pliable growing stage when the antlers are in velvet, particularly if the unusual configuration is only on one side. Atypical antlers may be due to a genetically inherited trait, especially if the unusual configuration is bilateral (Furtman 102). An example of this would be palmated antlers which have a somewhat flattened or webbed configuration where the antlers branch. Health and nutrition can also affect the growth and characteristics of the antlers. According to Geist, the excessive toxicity of summer forage can result in asymmetrical configuration of antlers (131).

June 29, 2001: A Wildlife Watching Day!

It was 4:29 a.m. and I was off again to Elk Country, still determined to see some calves, but reminding myself to appreciate whatever was given to me that day. At daybreak, when I was driving along Gray Hill Road, I saw several white-tailed deer as well as three bull elk in velvet.

These bulls were not nearly as chummy as the bulls in Benezette and Medix Run. They were more leery of human presence and did not like it when I got out of my vehicle to take their picture. They quickly crossed the road and disappeared into the misty meadow. That was the first time I had seen elk along Gray Hill Road.

Calves in Hiding

Where were the mama cows and calves? Finally, I asked Linda at the Benezette Store. I was told that most of them were in the "backcountry" having their calves at this time of the year. I took a long drive out along Hicks Run, but there were no elk to be seen. I opted not to hike on the trails alone. I didn't want to disturb the cow elk and the newborn calves. That was what I rationalized. Also, I didn't want to accidentally come across a calf and have a cow elk get upset with me. The truth is, I'm a scaredy cat!

A Healthy Fear

Why am I more afraid of a cow elk with a calf than a bull elk with large antlers in velvet? Animal behavior influenced by hormones and natural instincts can be somewhat unpredictable. The maternal instinct is a strong one and I had read that a cow elk would defend her calf by lashing out at a perceived predator with her sharp hooves. A bull in velvet, on the other hand, has antlers that are not yet hardened, and his main focus is on feeding continually to increase body mass and to grow large antlers. In early summer, a bull elk is neither aggressive nor competitive. But a bull in rut in September and October is, on the other hand, a primary example of an unpredictable, hormone-driven creature. So, given that information, I'm less afraid of a bull elk than a cow elk in the summertime and more afraid of a bull elk in autumn.

Sometimes fear is a good thing for an elk watcher to have. It can keep you safe and out of trouble! Fear can represent a profound respect for the animal and its strength. It's not a bad thing. In fact, I'm comfortable with it.

I'm happy to say that neither a bull elk nor a cow elk has ever charged me, but I have talked to people who have been charged by bull elk. Observing caution is important. Being scared is prudent. Repeat after me: The behavior of wild animals is often unpredictable.

Stomping, Snorting, Kicking White-Tails

White-tailed deer fawns are so "fawney" to watch as they cavort and frolic in the woods and meadows, observing humans with wide-eyed curiosity, and sometimes throwing caution to the wind, declaring their youth and innocence. But there is an exception to every assumption and I met up with such a fawn this morning.

I drove up to one of my favorite flowering food plot meadows, hoping to see some cow elk and calves. The fog had not yet lifted on the hill, and I walked slowly and quietly to the edge of the meadow. Alas! No elk were in the meadow, but there was a white-tailed doe and a fawn romping around her. The doe was grazing and did not notice me. Her offspring caught my movement and, out of curiosity, raced in my direction. Then the fawn stopped suddenly, stood still, and watched me for about 20 seconds. Then it squared its back and shoulders, flattened its ears, stomped its right front foot, and gave an arrogant snort. Suddenly it turned and kicked up both back legs and bolted in the opposite direction, away from its mother, and into the foggy mist!

With all the fussing of the fawn, the doe finally noticed my presence, and seemed to blame me that her youngster had taken off out of her sight! She glared at me, squared her back and shoulders, flattened her ears, and took four or five slow, stealthy steps in my direction as if she were about to pounce on me. She then stomped her foot several times, gave a loud startling snort and turned and flew her white flag tail at me. As she took off, she, too, kicked up both of her hind hooves! Whew! Like mother, like fawn! I know where that young one got its instincts! This pair put on a display that I wish Mike could have been there to witness! I was surprised, fascinated, and even startled by their snorts and stomps. White-tailed deer behavior can be as surprising and interesting to watch as elk behavior, but the moments are often fast and fleeting. Baby elk I did not see, but that stomping doe and feisty fawn sure put on a show for me on that fair June morning!

Creatures Great and Small

As I drove around Winslow Hill and Dewey Road, small cotton-tailed rabbits seemed to pop out of the weeds everywhere along the road. The meadow on the right side of Dewey Road had been recently mowed, and the bunnies were hopping around looking for new cover. Chipmunks scooted across the road. Sparrows sang symphonies in the bushes, and an occasional red squirrel raced across the landscape. Critters abounded along the roadside that day. They play a major part of my enjoyment of the elk range. The sights and sounds of all the busy little creatures add to the ambiance of elk country. Even the beautiful orange butterflies which like to pause on the flowering milkweed plants along Winslow Hill Road were a pleasure to behold, and were deserving of a couple of photographs! I figured a butterfly in the hand is worth two elk in the bush!

Beyond Youngmark Road, a small group of four cow elk and three spike yearlings were grazing. There were no new calves in this group, and no obviously pregnant cows. This may have been a group of yearlings temporarily abandoned by their mothers who had gone off alone to give birth and to keep their new calves in hiding for two weeks. The antler spikes on the male yearlings were obvious now. Young bulls usually remain with the cow group until their second autumn, which would be their first rut.

The Great Blue Heron

One of the best treats of the day was a drive out West Hicks Run Road. On the State Forest Lands is a refuge area and bird sanctuary. My SUV rumbled along the washboard ridges in the dirt road. I rolled down the windows to take in the sounds and smells of the forest. Suddenly on my right, a gigantic bird with a white and buff neck and chest, and blue-gray wings and head, stretched out his long neck, spread his great wings and rose from the bank of the creek! It made a loud, unusual call and I heard the swooshing sound of its massive wings as it took off. I thought it must be a crane of some type. Later, upon checking *Peterson's Field Guide to the Birds*, I found out that it was a "great blue" heron. I had seen plenty of "little blue" herons, which actually look gray, in ponds and streams in Pennsylvania and western New York, but never had I seen a great blue heron take off! It was phenomenal. The difference between a little blue heron and a great blue is equivalent to the difference between a Pennsylvania white-tailed deer and an elk! Get the picture?

Conversation at the Elk Country Store

I stopped in to say hello to Pat and Ken Rowe, the owners of the Elk Country Store in Medix Run since March 2001. I excitedly told them about the big bulls we'd been seeing just up the road, the "crane," which I later learned was a great blue heron, and the stomping, snorting, kicking fawn and doe. Pat told me about the bull elk they had seen in their yard, the rattlesnake that was killed on Rt. 555, and the black bear that some folks had seen earlier that day. It was hard to believe that this conversation was about things that were happening in

Pennsylvania, right in the yard, or just up the road! But then I remembered we were in elk country! Wildlife and the good life abound here! It is unique and wonderful indeed! Although snakes and bears are formidable, for the most part, the wildlife found here is wonderful and fascinating. And, of course, the elk are inevitably the main topic of conversation. Pat and Ken are learning that life in elk country is an ongoing adventure, with many stories to hear and to tell.

Two Broods of Turkeys Crossing the Road

On my way back home, traveling up the winding old Caledonia Road toward Rt. 255, I spotted what looked like two young turkeys on the left side of the road! Behind them, the hen emerged with six more chicks. They proceeded to cross the road in single file in front of me. It reminded me of grade school! I decided to try for a photo, but the hen was too efficient in getting her brood hidden and dispersed in the tall weeds on the other side of the road. When I got into my vehicle to drive away, it was déjà vu, all over again! There was a second brood of seven turkeys and a hen on the left side. They proceeded to cross the road in front of me. This time, I was confident I could get a photo, but when a car approached from the other direction, the turkeys scrambled quickly into cover and were seen no more, and I was left holding the camera. I decided I'm too slow to be photographing quick subjects. I'll stick with elk.

Reflections on a Beautiful Day

I decided that day that I enjoyed visiting the elk range in the summertime every bit as much as in autumn, and perhaps more so, because it was so exquisitely beautiful, and so filled with unexpected joys and surprises.

There is a poem I remember from my younger days:
Love each living thing,
Both the whole and every grain of sand,
And if you love each thing,
You will perceive the mystery of God in all.
(Author unknown)

Every visit to the Pennsylvania Elk Range is that kind of an experience for me. I'm grateful for every butterfly, every flowering plant, every elk, every turkey, and every cotton-tailed rabbit. In the appreciation of each thing, I marvel at the wondrous ways of the awesome God who created it all.

July 7, 2001: Bulls in Cameron

Mike and I thought it would be fun to drive down to the elk range from the northeast side for variety, taking Rt.120 from Emporium to Driftwood. As we drove through the village of Cameron at 7:11 a.m., two bull elk with huge, velvet-covered antlers were feeding in a grassy lawn on the left-hand side of the road. We realized immediately that these were wild elk, not acclimated to being around humans. Even stopping the car and opening the door a good distance from where they were feeding put them on alert. They scrutinized my movements the entire time. They began a slow retreat toward the woods, but not before I got an impressive photo.

Cows and Butterflies

A lone cow was feeding along Rt. 555 and we wondered if she had a calf hidden somewhere in the vicinity. When we reached Winslow Hill, we saw no elk in the flowering clover meadow, but there were three cow elk grazing and browsing on forage right by the road just beyond the Scenic Elk Viewing

Area. Five or six orange butterflies were poised on the lavender flowers of the milkweed plants nearby. I paused in the quiet, and listened to the chewing sounds of the feeding cows, and the rustling of the bushes as they walked along.

How I love the sights and sounds of elk country!

Elk Path Processions

As Mike and I started walking out on a path extending to the south side of the hill, he reminded me not to step up on the piles of wood, logs, brush, and rocks adjacent to the path, since snakes sometimes make their home in such an environment. He didn't have to tell me twice. I'll stick to the elk path! As we walked out on the path that led through the high grass and along the ridge with an open view of the entire hillside, the birds began calling loudly. I thought, if there were any elk out there, the birds have already alerted them to our presence. We didn't see any elk, but all along the path were plenty of elk droppings and hoof prints.

Seeing the worn narrow path reminded me of an elk behavior that I find absolutely fascinating. Elk frequently move in single file when traveling through the woods or moving from one feeding ground to another. Often an experienced matriarch cow leads the procession.

During the previous summer when we were near Jackson Lake in the Grand Teton National Park on a June evening, just as the sun had gone down we watched a large group of cows, calves, and yearlings moving through the willows, in a single-file line that appeared endless. We observed this from a vantagepoint on a rocky bluff. I stopped counting at 95 elk, and they were still coming into the grassy knoll to feed. It was truly an awesome, breath-taking procession, something I will never forget.

There are many well-worn, narrow elk paths in Pennsylvania elk country. They are used regularly by the elk as they move from place to place in search of food. The time of this movement most often corresponds to daybreak or dusk.

The groups of elk moving along the paths may not be as large as the herds in the Tetons, but certain instinctive elk behaviors and habits are as apparent in the elk here in Pennsylvania as they are in the western states.

July 14, 2001: Back Together Again

I set out on the 65 mile drive to the elk range on this clear Saturday morning in hopes of seeing some cow elk with growing young calves. I figured that by now most of them would have returned from the "backcountry" with gangling calves in tow, and regrouped with other cows, nursing calves and yearlings. This time, they were there to be found, in an open field above Youngmark Road.

The group was busy and animated. The mother cows were back with their new offspring and reunited with their lonely yearlings. There were seven cows and yearlings, and three calves feeding in the meadow. The calves trotted gingerly but never strayed far from their mothers. There was also a pair of twin fawns playing near the elk nursery group. The meadow was noisy as you might expect a nursery to be, as the mothers and calves chirped sounds to each other. The eyes of the cow elk were on their own offspring, even as the fawn sideshow took place. Two spike bull yearlings also started running and cavorting together. They galloped and pranced back and forth and around the entire meadow. They looked like they were having a game of tag! The small herd appeared happy to be together once again. I'm not sure what those fawns were celebrating – life would be my guess.

"Sarah, Plain and Tall"

Across Winslow Hill Road from the Scenic Elk Viewing Area, I spotted two cows and a yearling spike bull. One of the cows was the tallest I have ever seen on the elk range! Her legs were like stilts! I estimated that she was at least five feet high at the shoulder. She was stately and simply lovely. So I named her Sarah, after the character in the movie, "Sarah, Plain and Tall." I watched her browse her way down the hill and out of my sight.

The Cow With Earrings and a Necklace

I drove into the entrance of the Scenic Elk Viewing Area on SGL 311 to check out a cow browsing on the tender budding shoots of the bushes. As I climbed the small grade and looked over, there was another cow. One of them had a yellow radio collar and a round yellow button attached to each ear. It looked like she was dressed up for a party! There she was, all dolled up, but there would be no dating for her until September! I figured that this cow must be part of a research study, and that her "jewelry" was necessary for telemetry monitoring.

After I took her picture, a truck pulled up. The driver was a friendly gentleman named Carl with a hat that said, "Glacier National Park." We quickly got into conversation about the West, including Yellowstone and Alaska. He had just returned from a trip to Alaska and Glacier National Park in Montana. We talked about the elk and the importance of habitat land, and we exchanged reports about the wildlife we had seen on the elk range that day. He had seen a big bull in town and several flocks of wild turkeys on the food plots near Dewey Road. He enjoys photographing the elk, and figured that I must really like them as well, since I was walking up on the dirt hill just to get a picture of a cow. While we talked, another cow approached from the opposite direction and silently and cautiously walked around our vehicles to join the other cows on the small hill.

What I learned that morning is that there are other people like myself, who really love and appreciate the elk and enjoy them immensely. Carl is one of them. I hope I'll get to see his elk photographs someday.

Wild Turkeys on the Food Plot

I had almost forgotten about the wild turkeys that Carl had told me about earlier, when I noticed a truck pulled off on the side of Dewey Road overlooking the expansive field located there. The people were watching several broods of wild turkeys poking around on the food plot. I guess I also forgot that turkeys are not acclimated to the presence of humans the way some of the elk seem to be. When I got out of my car and stood on a small rise to take their picture, they started turkey-talking gibberish and all of a sudden the whole group flushed! Oops. That was the end of the turkey watching that day for me as well as the people in the other truck. I sheepishly got back into my vehicle and avoided eye contact with anyone. When you scare away the animals, there is nothing left to watch. The only consolation is, I learned a lesson from my mistake: Turkeys apparently don't like to have their picture taken while they are eating!

The Big Bull Downtown

At the bottom of Winslow Hill Road, in town, adjacent to the tavern was an enormous 9 x 10 bull elk grazing and wandering through the yards of the nearby houses. His antlers bent like they were made of rubber when he brushed them from side to side against some tree branches. It appeared that the velvet was itchy and he just had to scratch that itch! Within a few more weeks, the antlers would be completely hardened and the velvet would begin to be rubbed off. When the antlers are fully-grown, the bone mineralizes or hardens and the blood supply to the velvet skin covering the antlers decreases, becomes itchy, and dies. Usually this happens in late August. Also during the summer, insects are incessantly biting the tender velvet skin, which is very rich in blood supply and nerve endings. The resultant itching is sometimes tormenting to the elk. Whatever the cause of the itching on that mid-July morning, those pliable velvet antlers were getting a good scratching.

Since mature bulls grow their best antlers when they are between seven and twelve years of age, I figured that the downtown bull must be in that general age range. In the book *Elk Country*, Valerius Geist says, "Huge antlers are often asymmetrical and are carried by bulls in the later third of their life (47)." From this information, it may be safe to assume that the big bull downtown is in the later third of his life, since his antlers were huge and asymmetrical.

Velvet Air Conditioners

Bull elk have their own built in air-conditioners during the summer months. The velvet skin covering of the antlers is very rich in blood supply. When outside air and breezes flow through the antlers, it cools the blood flowing through the velvet. The cooled blood is then circulated throughout the rest of the body. This bull elk was sporting top-of-the-line air-conditioning units! His rack was a 9 x 10. Of course, the air-conditioners only work when the velvet is covering the antlers.

Horns Vs. Antlers

Although some people use the terms "horns" and "antlers" interchangeably, there are very distinct differences between the two. Antlers are made of living tissue which hardens into bone; they are grown and shed annually. Usually, antlers are grown by the male of the species. Caribou are an exception, since the females also grow antlers. Antlers typically have branches.

Horns, on the other hand, consist of a bony core covered with dead tissue called keratin, the substance in hooves, claws, and fingernails. Horns are permanent and are not shed. New growth rings of keratin are added annually. One exception to this is the pronghorn antelope, which sheds the outer sheath of its horns annually. Either males or females of a species can grow horns. Horns do not have branches.

Eli, the Newborn Elk Calf

During the morning, while following the large-antlered bull, I had the pleasure of meeting a wildlife photographer from Coudersport named Alan Thoms. He showed me some of his professional photographs, which included three pictures taken on June 7th of a newborn elk calf, and one of a bright-eyed, white-tailed deer fawn. They were beautiful photographs! One was of the elk calf I had dreamed of seeing that summer – a small, spotted, wide-eyed creature curled up in the ferns. I ended up purchasing the photo from Alan that day.

I proudly showed the beautiful 11" x 13" elk calf photograph to Ben and Janet, the owners of the Benezette Store, and to Sonya, a friendly teenager who works at the store. Later I also showed off the photo to Pat and Ken at the Elk Country Store in Medix Run, and to their friend Brenda, a volunteer from a chapter of the Rocky Mountain Elk Foundation. The marvelous photograph of the newborn calf curled up in the ferns would soon have a home on our living room wall! This was the baby elk I had been looking for, the picture that I never got to take in June. I named the calf Eli.

Alan had other elk photos in an album as well. Of course, looking at them just made me wish I owned a new camera with a big zoom lens! But then I'd also need a tripod to put it on. For now, I will stick to book writing and utilize the digital photos I have been accumulating for the past year and a half.

I figured I would get the calf picture double-matted and custom-framed. On the way home, I stopped at the WalMart in St. Marys, and there I found an oak frame, which just happened to match the frame of the bull elk picture in our living room! The double mats included with the frame were ivory and tan-colored and would suit this photograph perfectly, and I would save the cost of custom framing! Little Eli's picture earned a place of distinction on the pine-paneled wall of our rustic living room that very afternoon, appearing very much at home with the other wildlife décor, which includes "Bucky" (Mike's deer head), a moose tapestry, and a white-tailed buck afghan covering the sofa.

August 2001: Gigantic Antlers

Mike and I took a late afternoon drive down Rt. 120 from Emporium to Driftwood and then turned onto Rt. 555. Just a short distance from Driftwood, we spotted a bull lying in the front yard of a house trailer! He was next to the bicycle at the bottom of the wooden steps to the front entrance. At first, Mike thought it was lawn art, and not a real bull! Then the bull slowly moved his head! His 8 x 9 antlers were silhouetted against the white siding and he was a splendid sight to behold. He seemed right at home! My zoom lens captured a nice photograph of this bull.

When we got to Benezette, we stopped at the store and I got my cherry ice pop, so I knew what would happen next. As we started up Winslow Hill Road, we spotted two large bulls in a lawn on the left. It was a Saturday and there were lots of people on the elk range. We parked in the parking lot of the church, and Mike waited in the car while I walked along the road to take a photograph. One bull was lying in a yard next to a 55-gallon drum. I took the photo to show the size comparison. The bulls looked heavy now, as they continued to increase their body weight and size in preparation for the approaching rut. Their antlers were huge, and I wondered how much longer it would be before they started rubbing off the velvet.

One of the bulls we were watching appeared to be a mature bull with very thick antlers. He was a 9 x 10. I had read in Murie's writings that the mature older bulls, who had shed their antlers as early as February and were the first to start growing the new velvet, would be among the first to have their antler growth completed, after which the velvet would be rubbed off.

The hardened antlers of a mature bull elk usually weigh between 24 and 40 pounds. In very large bulls, some sources estimate antlers make up one-third of the total skeletal weight of the bull. Now that's a big bunch of bones!

Rubbing Off the Velvet

When the growth of the antlers is completed, they become hardened into bone. Then the velvet skin covering begins to die. The bull begins to rub off the velvet covering by thrashing and rubbing his antlers on tree limbs and bushes. Bloody velvet strips are seen hanging from his full-grown antlers. The velvet may be entirely removed within a twenty-four hour period. The small ridges you can see running along the length of the bony antlers are the channels previously occupied by the blood vessels in the velvet covering. Alas, his air-conditioner is broken! And the rut is about to begin!

Sparring

Prior to the rut, and after the velvet is removed from the antlers, sparring matches between bulls of similar size frequently take place. They will lock antlers and push each other back and forth. Sparring is a physical conditioning workout that builds strength and skill in preparation for the real head-to-head combat that occurs during the rut. Besides strengthening the bulls for more serious antler engagements, sparring is also a preliminary way of determining the hierarchy among bulls in advance of the rut (Furtman 94).

Besides sparring with other bulls, a bull will spar with small trees and bushes. In addition, he will put on intimidating displays for rivals by prodding the ground with his antlers, and lifting and scattering clods of dirt and grass which he will sometimes carry around on his antlers. This activity also serves to polish the antler tips, which will remain a whitish color.

In this process of sparring and physical conditioning, the neck of a bull elk becomes enlarged as increasing hormone levels enhance muscular development. The neck musculature is strengthened by constantly supporting his heavy headgear. Just carrying around a large rack of antlers provides a continual weight-training workout.

Scent Rituals

During the rut, the bulls engage in pheromonious or odorous behavior rituals. One of these behaviors is called "wallowing." The bull will use a shallow muddy hole or will create his own by pawing the ground with his hooves and prodding it with his antlers. He will then urinate in it and roll in it. Covering his neck and body with the muddy mixture makes the rutting bull appear even bigger and more formidable than he already is. In addition, wallowing serves to cool the bull during the rut. This is a bonus because the bull no longer has the velvet skin covering his antlers to serve as a circulatory cooling mechanism. Most of all, wallowing is a way of utilizing scent to broadcast his presence and readiness to mate.

Additionally, the elk have scent glands, called preorbital glands, located near each eye. As he rubs his face, neck, and antlers on small trees, he deposits scent from these glands as well as scent from the mud-soaked urine caked to his neck hair

(Geist 91). These activities serve to mark the bull's territory and to advertise his availability for mating.

When a bull makes grunting or chuckling sounds at the end of bugling, he bends his neck down and directs a spray of his own urine to his neck hair (Geist 91). His musky urine is used much like cologne or aftershave to attract and impress the female of the species. Whew! He'd be hard to miss!

September 18, 2000: A Pause in the Rut

September is always a busy month at the college where I work. That makes it all the more important for me to take the time to make the trip to Benezette to see the elk and listen to the bugling. Elk watching for me is both relaxing and exhilarating. It's like a tonic that decreases stress and increases energy. There is nothing quite like a therapeutic dose of elk country.

Before the sun went down in elk country, Mike and I heard the bugling calls bouncing and echoing through the valley. I took a walk along the road by Grant Hill. The thrashing sounds of twigs snapping and bushes rustling caught my attention. Out of the thicket nearby emerged a very impressive bull elk with an 8 x 7 rack of antlers, polished to perfection! I could see him easily from where I was standing and didn't need to get any closer. I was so nervous that I couldn't hold my camera still, and the photos I took came out blurry. Then, the big bull dropped to his knees and lay down in the open field. I was impressed that he knelt to say his prayers first. That's a good boy! It was then that I got a spectacular zoomed-in photo of him with his head held high, looking very regal. Majestic is a fitting descriptor for this bull. One of my favorite elk photos to this day is the one I took of that bull lying down in the field on Grant Hill, taking a time-out early in the rut.

Further up the road, there were cars parked and people walking up the bank to an open field. In the wooded thicket behind the field, a couple more bulls were lying down resting. An enormous amount of energy is expended by bulls during the mating season. Some large bulls lose as much as one hundred pounds of body weight during the rut. They will rest to conserve energy whenever possible. These bulls did not have harems of cows. Perhaps they had already been defeated by competitors and were taking a break before embarking on another bugling tour. With some exceptions, only the herd bull will mate with the cows in a harem. Some challengers and younger bulls will get their chance later in the rut as the older herd bulls wear out. Some may even be successful in stealing a cow from a harem. We heard an occasional bugle in the distance.

We met a friendly five-year-old girl named Kylie who was visiting the elk range with her grandparents from Uniontown. She got to take the day off from preschool to go on the trip. She talked softly to us as well as to the elk, and asked her grandpa many questions.

I observed as other people abandoned common sense and walked dangerously close to the bulls, just to get a photograph. Even though the bulls were lying down, they can get up quickly and can run at a speed of thirty miles per hour any time they please. Rut is definitely not the season to test them.

Bull elk have been known to charge people during the rut. Even the "friendly" bull elk in Benezette do not always behave as people might expect. Common sense tells me to stay back!

Whenever I have a gut feeling that I should use caution, I follow my gut feeling. Better to err on the side of caution than to suffer a punctured lung from a sharp antler to the ribs! I have never regretted investing in a camera with a zoom lens.

On the other side of the road, a spike bull was thrashing the tar out of a small evergreen tree. He gave quite a demonstration. He must have been honing his skills for future years when his antlers would be large and he would be a contender in the rut. Instinct driven behavior is fascinating to watch. But that was the end of the small evergreen tree!

Watching for Elk!

It was another beautiful September afternoon as we headed down the road to elk country. Today was special because Mike and I were taking our friend Donny Johnson to see the elk for the first time. As we headed up Winslow Hill about an hour before sunset, I said a little prayer that we would see elk – lots of elk – and that Donny would have the thrill of seeing some of them up close.

We reached the crest of the hill and the scenic overlook at the Gilbert Tract near Dewey Road. A short distance before Winslow Hill Road makes a sharp right bend, we pulled off of the road to look for elk. There was a rustling of branches and up from the wooded slope stepped a cow elk, which proceeded to walk across the road and eat the apples that had fallen from a tree overhanging the road. As she strolled along the asphalt, she came very close to our parked vehicle, and needless to say, we were all delighted! That was Donny's first close-up sighting of an elk.

It was still daylight and a truck with two young guys in it approached very slowly from the other direction. Both the driver and the passenger had their eyes turned in the direction of the scenic view and did not notice the cow in the road until they nearly bumped into her! On their faces were looks of disbelief, relief, and delight. That was an elk encounter they will not soon forget! Fortunately, it turned out all right. The moral of the story is this: As you eagerly search the hillside for elk, watch out for the one walking right in front of you!

The Bonfire and the Bugling

When we reached the bottom of Winslow Hill in Grant, we stopped to say hello to our friends, Bill and Bobbi. We took a short walk up the road to watch a couple of cow elk feeding on some apples in a lawn nearby. Bill had built a bonfire and we all sat around it as the twilight turned to darkness. Back and forth across the valley came the resonating bugling calls of two or three bull elk. Donny would remind us to "Listen!" each time he heard it, which was about every five to seven minutes. In the next yard, three cow elk were grazing in the lawn. One of them triggered a motion sensor light and we enjoyed watching the cows in the spotlight from our front row seats beside the warm and glowing campfire. The air was brisk and the smoke added a soothing aroma. The bugling sounds and the burning logs took my thoughts eons away from the busy workweek. I couldn't help but think of the Native Americans of the tribes of long ago, sitting around a campfire and listening to the bugling of the wapiti in autumn. That night in Grant, life was good.

We returned home late, tired but content, and full of anticipation for what Donny would tell everyone at work the following day. He excitedly gave a full report to everyone at the university who would listen. He included the number of elk seen (24), the number of white-tailed deer seen (37), and a description of the bugling we heard. He gave the full account of the cow that triggered the motion sensor light while we sat by Bill's bonfire, and the cow that had been eating apples in the road right next to our vehicle on Winslow Hill. What's so great about Donny is that he has a mind for details and is great at keeping track of things. He also has a wonderful enthusiasm for sharing his joy and excitement with others. Since that day, he has called me the Elk Lady.

Mating Behavior

When a bull elk bugles, it is a mating call to the cow elk. When cows approach, the bull tries to impress them with his large body size, his scent, his enormous and well-polished antlers, and his bugling ability. It is his way of "strutting his stuff." His large size and antlers indicate that the bull not only has desirable genetic traits to pass on to offspring, but also that he has the ability to find adequate feeding areas. The bull will attempt to herd cows into a group called a harem. It is his collection of cows that he keeps on hand for the mating season. Calves accompany their mothers in the harem. Usually harems are kept in an open area where the harem master or herd bull can keep a close eye on them. He patrols the edges of the harem to protect his cows from other bulls in the vicinity. Also, he protects the cows from the pestering of younger bulls. Once in the harem, the herd bull will prevent the cows from straying or running off with another bull. Sometimes he will nip her hindquarters or poke her with an antler as a reminder of who is the boss.

Usually, yearling cows will be gathered into a bull's harem in the fall, even though most will not mate until the following autumn. On one occasion, Mike and I were watching a cow elk, probably a yearling, feeding alone in September. She curiously eyed us as she turned her cup-shaped ears in our direction. Then from a hillside behind her came the bugling call of a bull elk. She rotated her left ear toward the sound, listening, at least half-heartedly, to the bull's serenade. Maybe next year she would take more of an interest in the rut. This season, she seemed more interested in chomping on apples.

Yearling spike bulls stay with the cows until the autumn of their first rut, when they are a year and four months old. At that time, the herd bull and harem master will chase them out as he gathers and protects his harem. Young calves are allowed to stay. Sometimes the young spike bulls will try to stay on the edge of the harem. They are accustomed to being a part of the group, and at a young age, they are unable to compete for breeding rights. Also, most are not yet motivated by the strong breeding instincts of the mature herd bulls (Murie 123-24). Some of them don't even bother to rub the velvet off of their small antlers. Spikes rarely breed, but there are some exceptions.

Two-year-old bulls, on the other hand, are a completely different story, according to Murie (124). They try to steal cows from the harem and they pester the cows continually (Murie 124), until the herd bull drives them away. Their persistent efforts to breed are sometimes successful.

The largest and strongest bulls compete for position in the

hierarchy of the herd, and may challenge each other for control of a harem and breeding rights. Such challenges are not frequent but they do occur. Before resulting in antler-locking combat, bulls will put on dominance displays for one another to prove who is the biggest and the best. They will bugle loudly, run side-by-side and put on as ominous a show as possible. Sometimes one of the bulls will back off in retreat before any antler clashing occurs. But on occasion, in the heat of the rut, a real battle can ensue, leaving one of the bulls injured or even killed. Antler clashes don't last long, but are intense and seem longer than they actually are. This is not to be confused with sparring matches which take place between bulls in August, just prior to the rut, or after the rut has finished.

With the autumn rut in full swing, the bulls have gathered harems of cows and calves. A bull will often keep his harem in an open field where he can observe them and protect them from other bulls. The female elk have an estrus or fertile period which only lasts 12 to 15 hours. That is the only time the cow will be receptive to the mating advances of the bull. If the cow does not mate and conceive during the first estrus, another estrus will occur in 21 days. Cow elk can have up to four estrus periods in the fall, but usually they will conceive during the first or second. Most young cows will have their first estrus when they are two years and four months old.

Through scent and the receptive behavior of the female, the bull elk knows when she is ready to breed. Mating occurs only with her consent. Within the harem, the bull will sometimes lick a cow elk's face or flanks in his amorous moments. If a cow is not ready to mate she will hold her head low and twist her head side to side and open and close her jaws rapidly as a signal to the bull to stop (Geist 101). The herd bull honors her wishes and turns and bugles away from her, affirming that she is in control (Geist 102). When the cow is in estrus, she accepts the bull's advances. Mating is very brief and usually takes place early in the early morning or in the evening.

Watching the Bulls and Their Harems

In early October, I took Donny and his mother Helen on a visit to the elk range. At the Scenic Elk Viewing Area on Winslow Hill, we saw lots of action for the very first time. For almost a year I had never seen an elk from that viewing area. But that October evening, there was a harem of 27 cows and calves, and two branch-antlered bulls visible in the clear cut. We watched the bulls prance, bugle, and run parallel side by side. At one point we were sure they were going to clash their antlers together, but then one bull backed off, and a confrontation was averted. This is more frequently the outcome of bull challenges on the elk range. Head to head combat expends a lot of energy that is needed for breeding. If dominance displays and bullying can avert a fight, it saves both bulls a lot of energy. Antler clashes are frequently avoided when the bulls are unevenly matched. Since many of the bulls have hung around together in bachelor groups all summer, they have a pretty good idea of who is the biggest before the rut begins.

Bulls eat very little during the rut but drink plenty of water. They become exhausted by herding, mating, fighting, and vigilant monitoring of the harem.

Back down along Rt. 555, there was a huge bull elk herding his cows around in a large open field. He nipped at the hindquarters of a cow elk who was straying on the edge of the harem. I noticed a bloody mark on her right flank.

The Bull and the White-Tails

Further down the road toward Medix Run, a massive antlered bull stood in a field, surrounded, not by cow elk, but by at least a dozen animated white-tailed does and fawns. One of the fawns ran between his legs! They pranced and hopped around him in the field in a surreal scene that reminded me of the childhood game, "Ring Around the Rosy."

The bull elk seemed very much at ease with the entire situation, or was so tired from the energy expenditure of the rut that he didn't care. It was an unexpected and unusual scene, recorded in my mind's eye, because it was quite dark, except for the occasional illuminating glint of headlights passing the field.

Donny, Helen, and I were quite amazed at what we had seen in elk country that evening. As I drove down the road, suddenly out of nowhere, a white-tailed deer was in front of my headlights! By a miracle, I was able stop in time and did not hit it.

I'm convinced we had the protection of angels that night. I always pray for the protection of angels on all my trips to elk country. That night was no exception. And all three of us were thankful for that protection.

October 1, 2000: The Little Mus-Koose

It was a glorious autumn morning as I set out in the dark at 5:30 a.m. for elk country. Mike was in Wyoming on a hunting trip with his friend Larry. They had been selected to hunt mule deer and were away for the week. So it was the perfect time for me to make an early morning trip to Pennsylvania elk country. I was hoping for a less crowded elk watching experience today. I watched the first light enter the morning sky as I approached St. Marys and continued on to Benezette.

At 7:10 a.m. it was barely light enough to get a photo of an elk calf nursing. The lone cow elk and calf were in a field right along Rt. 555 near Grant as the morning mist was starting to lift. The calf must have been born late in the season because it was smaller than other calves I had seen earlier this fall. The mother cow must have conceived during a late estrus in the previous fall season. They were not part of any harem.

Late born elk calves are at a disadvantage in size going into the winter season. Young elk must have adequate body mass and fat stores to survive their first winter. Most of them will weigh close to 225 pounds before the winter season begins.

Later that day, as I drove back along the same road, I saw the same calf nestled in some weeds beside the road, and was able to take a photo without disturbing it. Besides the Shawnee word "wapiti," another Native American name for elk is "Mus-Koose" (Krakel 6). So I named him or her Little Mus-Koose, a very fitting name for a small elk calf.

A Morning Walk with a Monarch

I drove up Winslow Hill to the Scenic Elk Viewing Area. The fog was too thick to view the scenic hillside at that early hour. I got in the car and as I was pulling out, I heard the sound of bugling. As I drove ahead, the sound became stronger. I pulled off of the road, parked my vehicle and walked up the road. Up ahead, another car was parked and a couple of people were walking. They had been watching a bull elk on the left side of the road, behind the red house with the satellite dish, but it had wandered back into the woods.

As I was walking back to my car, I heard a bugle coming from the right side of the road. Another elk watcher said excitedly, "He's coming up the hill right over there!" I heard the rustling of the bushes and then, out of the thicket at 8:23 a.m. emerged a branch-antlered bull in all his regal spendor, less than ten yards from where I stood! He took my breath away! My, oh, my! He was an 8 x 9 bull. A bull with 6 or more points on each antler is called a "royal" bull. A "monarch" has at least

7 points on each side, and an "imperial" bull has 8 or more points on each antler ("Anatomy"). This bull was actually an "imperial" by that definition, and he was a monarch by poetic license. "A Morning Walk With a Monarch" sounded better to me than "A Morning Walk With an Imperial!"

He walked regally along the side of the field at a distance of about twenty feet, parallel to the road. I talked to him as he paused to graze, periodically bugle, and stare across the field into the foggy mist. He seemed oblivious to the fact that I was taking his picture over and over. People began to gather at the awesome spectacle. He was just traveling along, singing his song, and we walked parallel, "side by side." I watched him browse on the bushes and peek around the trunk of a large tree. He bugled again, and moved on, stepping over tree limbs, grazing his way through the grassy fields and into the lawns near the camps along Winslow Hill. Finally he decided to cross the road. There were cars parked everywhere by this time, but I was still able to get a picture of him trotting along flicking his tongue just before he crossed and wandered back behind Mountain Paradise Camp and into the woods at 9:11 a.m.

I still could not believe it! I had accompanied this monarch on his morning walk for 48 minutes, and for a distance of about half a mile. It was incredible! What a privileged experience. It is one I will never forget. Some of the photographs I took of him that morning are among my best. In fact, my favorite photograph of that regal bull elk graces the cover of this book! I am so grateful for that wonderful and memorable experience in elk country. My adrenaline was pumped up for the rest of the day! I excitedly returned to the Scenic Elk Viewing Area and showed the photos on my digital camera to anyone who was interested in seeing them. When I stopped at the Benezette store, I did the same thing. In fact, I met two women from Erie who had come to Benezette to see the elk. That was a nice coincidence because I was born and raised in Erie. I showed them the elk photos until the battery in my camera ran down.

When I returned to Bradford, I e-mailed photos of my

bugling buddy to Mike in Wyoming. Everyone out there was very impressed. Meanwhile, Larry had shot a mule deer and so had Mike! But I got an 8 x 9 bull elk…with my camera!

October 14, 2000: Rut Winding Down

I knew there would never be another elk watching experience quite like the one I had two weeks ago, but I was ready for whatever new experiences awaited me on another early morning visit to the elk range. The autumn foliage was vibrant with color this week and I was hoping to get some nice photographs. The weather report predicted a very warm and sunny autumn day. Mike was going hunting for pheasants in McKean County. He loves bird hunting and has a plaque in his office that says, "Business Hours Subject to Change During Grouse Season." He wouldn't be home until around dinnertime.

In the yard of a house on Winslow Hill Road, a small harem of nine cows and calves and a herd bull were grazing. I pulled off on the side of the road at 8:16 a.m. and no other cars were anywhere in sight. I watched the bull looking intently at a swing hanging in the yard. I had heard about bulls getting their antlers tangled in the chains of swing sets, and was very glad when he walked by it without incident. The autumn leaves were in brilliant shades of red, yellow and rust. As I snapped photos of the small harem amidst the colorful foliage, I noticed another bull had come on the scene and was positioned on the edge of the woods to the left of the harem. The herd bull moved immediately but slowly in that direction to check out the newcomer. Without any confrontation, the herd bull turned back and moved his harem into the woods as the other bull looked on. Must be they knew each other. As the group moved out, only the small faces of the calves watched me curiously as I took another photograph. The rut was winding down and there was no bugling to be heard this morning.

Traffic Hazards on Winslow Hill

Meanwhile, by 8:51 a.m., many more cars had stopped in and along the road as people eagerly converged to take pictures, some of them walking into the yards of camps and houses. Then a large RV stopped in the road, opposite my parked vehicle. By doing so, he immediately blocked the movement of traffic in both directions. A large logging truck impatiently honked his horn behind the RV. Finally the fellow in the camper moved down the road, just as I was sure the log truck was going to plow right into my SUV! I learned a lesson that day: Even when you pull your own vehicle off of the road, be aware of what other people are doing. If someone else blocks the flow of traffic on a public road, it could place you or your vehicle at risk. When people are creating a traffic hazard or other unsafe situation, I get my vehicle and myself out of the area as quickly as I can.

The traffic hazard on that Saturday morning reminded me of another situation on a previous visit during an autumn evening. It was dark and there were carloads of people on Winslow Hill. At the crest of Winslow Hill by the Gilbert Tract where the road bends sharply to the right, a bull elk was nervously walking down one lane of the asphalt road. There was a fence on one side and a line of parked cars and slow moving bumper-to-bumper traffic on the other, which prevented the bull from moving out of the road. Car horns were honking and the crowd was noisy. I could see the bull was shaking as he walked briskly down the road. There was no easy escape. He was trying desperately to get out of the road, but cars and people kept blocking his path. This was elk watching at its worst! I wanted to rescue the nervous bull elk. The elk should not be subjected to stress by humans for the sake of a photograph or a closer look. This incident was very disturbing to me. I knew then and there that I was going to do something to try to educate elk watchers to help prevent such situations from occurring.

Shortly after that experience, I volunteered to be a part of the effort to educate visitors to the elk range, to make elk watching more enjoyable and safer for everyone, including the elk.

Colorful Autumn

The Pennsylvania foliage in October is unsurpassed in its beauty and splendor. I drove for a hour and a half on some of the back roads on the elk range and took some photos that were exquisite. Daytime, when the elk are not readily visible in the open areas, is the perfect time to travel the back roads and observe the kaleidoscope of color of the Pennsylvania forests. Enjoying the many wonders of elk country in autumn adds diversity to the trip as well as to my photo collection.

On my drive through the state game lands on the elk range, I became aware that small game season had begun. Hearing an occasional gun shot and seeing hunters garbed in orange reminded me of the importance of staying along the road and wearing blaze orange for safety while walking on the elk range during this time of the year.

October 24, 2000: Bull in Camouflage

It was a drizzling morning when Mike and I drove to the elk range and out Rt. 555. Beyond the turn for Dent's Run, we spotted some bulls walking along the old railroad grade. One came into a field of tall grass and we pulled off of the road and watched him with binoculars as he strolled and fed on browse. The one thing I noticed about this bull was the dark brown coloring of his antlers, as compared to other antlers we had seen which were considerably lighter brown in color. I had read that many elements influence the staining of antlers, including bark, sap, mud, dirt, and blood (Krakel 26). Also, the type of trees the elk rubs with his antlers determines the coloring to a large extent. Rubbing on certain alders produces darker staining and rubbing on conifers or evergreens results in a lighter coloring of the antlers (Murie 85). This bull had apparently rubbed on alders. His antlers blended in so well with the dark branches of the trees and bushes around him, and the beige tones of the high grasses in the field were similar in color to his grayish-beige winter coat which was already visible. It was nature's perfect camouflage.

Pheasant in Hiding

I always enjoy the short jaunt down Dewey Road to the turn-around and back up again. Near the bottom, I spotted a ring-neck pheasant hiding in the weeds. I was able to get a photo of him, with his eye behind a branch. I guess he thought that if he couldn't see me that I couldn't see him either. My camera proved otherwise.

Three Turkeys Trotting

On a short ride out Dent's Run Road to Belle's Draft and back, we saw a beautiful curious white-tailed deer standing serenely along the side of the road. We watched three turkeys trot across the dirt road and then climb a steep slope on the right. They are fast little climbers! But I'm still too slow to get a picture of a turkey! As my husband Mike says, a moving target is always harder to hit.

Winterlude
January 2, 2000: Amazing Elmer

Y2K had arrived and our computer was still working! Hooray! Our friend Elmer, who was the best man in our wedding, was visiting us from Pittsburgh on New Year's Day. His wife Kate had died unexpectedly just three weeks earlier. Needless to say, it was a challenging time for him, and it was a privilege to open our hearts and our home to Elmer. I cooked pork and sauerkraut in the crock-pot and we had good conversation until late into the evening.

The following day, no snow was in the forecast, so we decided to show Elmer the elk on his drive back to Pittsburgh. He enjoys bird watching and butterflies, and I knew he would enjoy seeing the elk. I led the way to Benezette in my vehicle with Elmer and Mike following. When we got to Caledonia, Elmer parked his van and we all road in our SUV up Rt. 555 to Benezette.

It was mid-afternoon and we drove around Winslow Hill to places where we had seen elk previously, but, alas, no elk were to be found. That was because our timing wasn't quite right. Then, after riding around for more than an hour, we spotted an elk far off on a hill on the right as we were driving back up Dewey Road. As the sun was going down, we realized we had to get Elmer going on his way to Pittsburgh. When we reached the bottom of Winslow Hill and Rt. 555, we spotted a group of twelve elk in the yard beside the house on the corner. One was eating out of the birdfeeder! We noticed that one of the bulls had had his antlers sawed off, and wondered what kind of trouble he had gotten himself into. One of the bulls walked along the side of the house, right beside the windows. Elmer kept saying, "It's amazing!" He was impressed at the size of the elk, the herd behavior we were observing, and our good fortune of seeing the elk at close range. We took photographs, and I chattered on and on about the elk, one of my favorite subjects! Then as we drove back down Rt. 555, we saw another small herd near Summerson Road.

We drove an amazed Elmer back to his van. He had thoroughly enjoyed the trip. After Mike gave him directions to I-80, he was off to Pittsburgh as we started our drive back to Bradford on that chilly but clear January evening in the new millennium.

I could hardly wait to get my photos developed and send copies to Elmer. But the pictures came back completely black with only the elk eyes showing up light on the photos! Dang! We'll have to savor that elk watching trip in our memories. I know Elmer will remember it.

March 3, 2000: A Lone Bull in Winter

Although I don't visit the elk range as frequently in the winter, I was eager to go on this trip to try out our new digital camera. There was snow on the ground and I was hoping the elk would be easier to see.

Mike and I found a herd of twenty-four elk bedded down in a field on Winslow Hill Road. Elk move as little as possible in the winter to conserve energy. We tried not to disturb the group as we paused to watch them with binoculars. We didn't get out of our vehicle.

We came upon a lone bull standing and pawing in the snow with his hooves in an area along Winslow Hill Road. He looked rather dapper in his heavy grayish-white winter coat. His dark mane looked like a fur collar snuggled around his neck. He reminded me of a reindeer. Ho, ho, ho! He was busy eating grass which had been buried in the snow and kept his head to the ground most of the time. Then he paused and lifted his head as if posing for the picture! Another photographer arrived on the scene and we were both able to take his photo in the fading daylight.

Winter Pelage, Wonderfully Made

The winter coat or pelage of the elk is unique and intricate in its design. It consists of two kinds of hair: woolly hair close to the skin to provide warmth, and thick long guard hairs covering the other hairs which provide insulation and protection from snow and rain. The guard hairs are like hollow cylinders filled with a honeycomb of air pockets. The arrangement of the guard hairs and the woolly undercoat provide insulation and warmth similar to a Gortex coat, but is undoubtedly better! Snow will settle on an elk's back without even melting due to the effectiveness of his insulated winter coat! Such intricate details of creation are profoundly amazing to me. Psalm 139 comes to mind:

> For it was you who formed my inward parts;
> You knit me together in my mother's womb.
> I praise you for I am fearfully and wonderfully made.
> Wonderful are your works;
> That I know very well.
> (NRSV Bible, Ps. 139.13-14)

During the winter, besides digging through snow to feed on grass, the elk enjoy feeding on acorns as well as twigs and certain types of bark. Their four-chambered stomachs accommodate the digestion of very coarse foods. These large animals must find adequate food supplies even in the winter in order to survive. Within the hierarchy of the herd, the largest, dominant animals feed first, leaving the smaller and weaker animals to forage for what is left. Survival of the fittest and strongest animals insures propagation of the species. With the exception of some lone bulls, the elk stay together in large groups throughout the winter for safety. During bad weather, they will bed down together under the cover of trees and wait out the storm.

Cows Carrying the Herd

I particularly admire the toughness and tenacity of the cow elk and the pivotal role they play in the life of the elk herd year round. Their constant vigilance insures the safety and protection of the herd from danger and predators. Besides the vital role of giving birth in the spring, cow elk must maintain a healthy pregnancy throughout the lean winter months. A wise and experienced matriarch cow will lead the herd to feeding grounds throughout the winter. She remembers where the acorns are buried in the snow, and where the best cover is to be found. This is learned behavior that comes from many years of following other matriarchs in the herd through many seasons of survival. All cows are matriarchs in training. The strongest, smartest, and most alert cows will become the leaders in future years. They will be the ones to teach their daughters, granddaughters and great granddaughters the basic techniques of herd survival. The cows will also guide and teach the young bulls during their first sixteen months, until the spike bulls go off on their own or team up with the other bulls to grow their antlers and to prepare for the rut. After the rut, the larger bulls retreat from the herd to rest and feed alone or with other bulls. The lonely spikes rejoin the herd.

On the Pennsylvania elk range, it is not uncommon to see bull elk rejoin the herd groups during the early months of winter. When a bull loses his antlers, he will go off on his own. The oldest bulls loose their antlers as early as February. Most bulls will lose them in March, and young bulls as late as April or May.

Chasing Antler Sheds

On the elk range, some people will track and follow bulls at that time of the year, in hope of picking up shed antlers. A pair of sheds is a prize indeed, since both are not usually shed in the same place and at the same time. If shed antlers remain in the woods without being recovered, creatures such as mice, squirrels, and porcupines will nibble the bony sheds for the calcium and other minerals they contain. Over time, the antlers will disintegrate and return their nutrients to the earth.

The Great Antler Auction

In Jackson, Wyoming, hundreds of shed elk antlers are piled thick and high to form massive arches on the four corners of a downtown square. Each year, the local boy scout troop collects the shed antlers on the elk refuge lands and holds a fundraising auction in that same town square. In his book, *Season of the Elk*, Dean Krakel II described this event called the Great Antler Auction. He stated that people come from all over the world come to bid on and win the coveted antlers, and one year, during frenzied bidding wars, more than $19,000 was raised (94). Some people disputed the idea of the auction money going to the local Boy Scout troop. Krakel said they believe that since the antlers were shed on federal land that everyone pays for with taxes, the antlers belong to everyone, not just the boy scouts. Others suggested that the money raised should go back into the cost of feeding the elk on the refuge (94). It seems that no matter where elk live, controversy of one kind or another seems to follow them. Today, the money raised is used to help subsidize the winter-feeding of the elk on the refuge in Jackson Hole.

Maybe someday Benezette will hold its own Great Antler Auction. Proceeds could be used to enhance the habitat on the elk range. But I'm certain there would be varying opinions on that idea. Until I acquire my own set of sheds, I'm hoping the "finders-keepers" rule stands.

The Sweet Promise of Springtime

The lengthening of daylight heralds the impending arrival of springtime, melting snow, and better food supplies for the winter-weary elk herd. Elk will lose a lot of body weight and fat reserves during the winter. Most vulnerable are the calves. Late winter storms can be especially hard on them. But if they can hang on until the growth of spring grasses begins and the tender leaves start growing on the bushes, a new season of plenty awaits them. The calls of the cow elk will soon be heard as springtime awakens and the wondrous cycle of life continues.

IV

ELK COUNTRY ISSUES

Those Blankity-Blank Elk

Not everyone loves the elk. The farmers suffer crop damage and subsequent financial loss and local residents lose trees, flowers, and shrubbery to these huge herbivores (plant eaters) which consume eight times more food per day than a white-tailed deer. Each day, on an average, an elk consumes approximately three pounds of food for each 100 pounds of body weight. That is a lot of vegetation, considering that a bull elk weighs an average of 700 pounds and a cow elk weighs an average of 500 pounds. Then they proceed to produce rich fertilizer in similarly large quantities.

Resolving crop damage conflicts with farmers and residents continues to be an ongoing challenge. The use of deterrent fencing, rubber pellets, relocating problem elk to the expanded range, continuing habitat improvements to keep elk off of agricultural land, and the planning of limited elk hunting seasons are approaches being utilized by the Game Commission to help resolve these problems.

Forgive Us Our Trespassing

Some residents have told me that the elk are not the problem. They love the elk; that is why they own camps or houses in elk country. Tourists are the problem, they say, because they create safety hazards and are sometimes an annoyance to local residents.

Being an elk watcher and frequent visitor to the elk range myself, I think that most visitors don't intend to break the rules or be an annoyance, but frequently they are not aware of the code of conduct. Many of them do what they see others doing, because they aren't sure of the rules or the limits. Of course, there are a few who don't use good judgment, set a bad example, and give the rest of the tourists a bad name! But I honestly believe that the majority of visitors are decent people who want to do the right thing. They just need more information ahead of time. Common sense helps, but so does information. Educating tourists about appropriate behavior on the elk range may be one strategy to help to improve the situation. And, of course, being a good example speaks volumes!

Courtesy and helpful communication on the part of local residents can go a long way toward creating a welcoming climate for tourists. The residents are experts of a sort, because they have lived with the elk. Their knowledge and expertise can be very helpful and of interest to visitors who enjoy learning about the elk and the local area. Also, from my experience, the majority of the local residents I've met truly love and enjoy the elk and are appreciative of the unique opportunity to live among them and share the land with them. They have many wonderful stories to tell.

Elk Hunting Reintroduced

With the elk herd healthy and thriving, the Pennsylvania Game Commission is attempting to balance elk population growth with habitat demands and the need to resolve the conflicts affecting local farmers and residents. Hunting will be utilized as an elk management strategy.

With the signature of Governor Thomas Ridge at the end of the year 2000, the State of Pennsylvania approved the Game Commission's request for a limited elk hunt for November 2001. The Board of Game Commissioners gave final approval to the first elk hunting season in Pennsylvania in 70 years.

For the hunters of Pennsylvania, the opportunity to participate in a limited elk hunt after a 70-year prohibition is a very exciting prospect, as well as a major historic event. A total of 30 licenses (15 for antlered elk and 15 for antlerless elk) were issued after the names were drawn by public lottery on September 29, 2001 at Pennsylvania's Elk Outdoor Expo 2001 on Winslow Hill in Benezette. A total of 50,697 applications were received; of these, 50,046 were eligible for the drawing for the 30 elk licenses for the 2001 elk hunting season. One woman and 29 men were among the selected hunters. There were applicants from every state except North Dakota and Hawaii, as well as from 8 different countries. A Vermont resident was the only out-of-state applicant that was drawn for a license.

Elk are among the largest and most desirable hunted big game animals in North America. The antlers alone are a coveted trophy, and from what I have heard, elk meat is tender, delicious, and nutritious, as well as low in fat. I was surprised to read that a 3 oz. leg cut of elk meat or elk venison was lower in cholesterol than skinless chicken which contains 72 milligrams, and equal in cholesterol to steamed halibut which contains 62 milligrams (Robb 144).

Even though Pennsylvania is a state where hunting has historically been and still is extremely popular and well accepted, there has been mixed sentiment about the hunting of elk in Pennsylvania. Some folks say it would be much like hunting a dairy cow — a slaughter rather than a hunt — because the unassuming elk near some of the villages on the elk range have become a bit too accustomed to the presence of people. This is not the case with the elk residing in the more remote woodland areas of the range; they are more leery of people and fit the description of wild elk. To address this concern, elk hunting will not be permitted within an eight square mile area in and near the village of Benezette, including the Scenic Elk Viewing Area on State Game Land 311 on Winslow Hill Road.

Some folks object, not to the hunting, but to the decision to make elk hunting licenses available to people from outside of the local area, and especially from outside of the state. The argument is that "outsiders and flat-landers should not be allowed to come in and shoot our elk, which eat our shrubs, trees and crops. If anyone is going to hunt them, it should be us." Nevertheless, many Pennsylvania hunters apply for and obtain out-of-state hunting licenses in other states in the country. It seems fair that Pennsylvania would reciprocate by offering at least a small percentage of elk hunting licenses to out-of-state applicants. Only two licenses were made available to out-of-state residents for the scheduled 2001 elk hunting season and only one out-of-state name was drawn. Sounds fair enough.

Some people consider the elk untouchable or off limits, perhaps because the native Pennsylvania elk herd became extinct. Others are simply against hunting or intentional killing of wildlife for any reason.

Still others worry that an elk hunt may be a bit premature, considering that the elk population dwindled to a frightening low of 38 in 1974, less than 30 years ago. With the availability of the additional land which constitutes the expanded elk range, some folks would like to have seen the herd reach the Game Commission's projected elk population maintenance goal of between 800 and 1,300 elk on the 835 square mile range before reintroducing hunting as a wildlife management strategy. Actually, the resilience and rapid growth of the herd from a population of 38 just 30 years ago, should be reassurance that taking 30 elk from the current herd of 700 should not negatively effect herd growth and expansion, but will help keep the population growth within manageable limits. Such management is important for the maintenance of adequate habitat and a healthy herd, and allows time for planned habitat enhancement to continue. Even after the scheduled elk hunt this fall, it is very likely that the herd population will approach 800 by next year, in light of the average annual elk population increase of 12-16%.

Some people are concerned that killing 15 large branch-antlered bulls could deplete the best breeding stock of the herd. Rawland D. Cogan, chairman of the Pennsylvania Elk Hunt Advisory Committee, stated prior to the drawing for the licenses that the reproductive capacity of the elk herd could actually be increased by the elimination of some of the older bulls. The effects of the elk hunt will be monitored and evaluated extensively.

There is no guarantee that all the bulls killed will be the biggest and best of the herd, although that would surely be the goal of most hunters. There is also no guarantee that 15 bull elk and 15 cow elk will be taken during the six-day hunting season in November, since each hunter is assigned to one designated area or section in which he or she is permitted to hunt.

Many people don't realize that most hunters care about and respect the wildlife which they hunt. Responsible hunters are very interested in conservation and the long-term maintenance of the populations of the species that they hunt so that the animals and the sport will be available to future generations as well. Hunters are among the biggest financial supporters of conservation and habitat enhancement programs nationwide through organizations such as the Rocky Mountain Elk Foundation, Ducks Unlimited, Ruffed Grouse Society, and the National Wild Turkey Federation, the Theodore Roosevelt Conservation Alliance, as well as state game commissions and other groups.

In proposing a limited elk hunt for November of 2001, the Pennsylvania Game Commission officials made a well-researched decision which they believe is in the best interest of conservation and maintenance of a healthy elk herd over the coming decades. Continued growth of the herd demands increased habitat. Enhancement of the elk range habitat requires funding, and the elk hunting application fees and licenses provide some of the revenue for this effort. In addition, hunting can serve to keep the size of the herd within manageable proportions as habitat enhancement continues. Consistent with its mission and goals, the Pennsylvania Game Commission can more easily justify continued financial support for the habitat of hunted species rather than for species that are not hunted. According to Cogan, who was the guest speaker at Pennsylvania's Elk Outdoor Expo 2001, the planned elk hunt, limited to thirty total licenses, represents an "ultra-conservative management approach."

V

LOOKING TO THE FUTURE

The Elk Watcher's Wish List:

It only takes one or two trips to the Pennsylvania Elk Range to realize that certain services are lacking which would increase enjoyment, safety, and convenience for visitors to elk country. These are the top three items on my Elk Watcher's Wish List:

- Spacious public restrooms with handicap accessibility in more than one location on the elk range are a necessity to accommodate the basic needs of tourists.
- A Visitor's Center with available maps and elk information, public restrooms, and an outdoor observation deck and picnic area would be a hospitable addition. A public indoor lodge with chairs, benches, a stone fireplace, and windows overlooking a scenic view of the elk range would be spectacular!
- Numerous designated paved pull-off areas on the sides of the roads would increase safety while elk watching.

The Pennsylvania Elk Watching and Nature Tourism Project

A project is underway to assess, plan, and fund strategies for improving services and accommodations and increasing tourism in elk country, while at the same time maintaining the natural beauty and integrity of the rural region. The following agencies are working cooperatively in this effort: the Pennsylvania Game Commission, the Department of Conservation and Natural Resources, the North Central Pennsylvania Regional Planning and Development Commission, and the USDA Forest Service

("Elk Watching Project"). Becoming involved and giving input into this effort is one way to maximize the benefits for residents and tourists as well as the elk. Similar efforts have benefited wildlife refuge areas and state and national parks across the country, and have been successful in raising public awareness and promoting financial support for wildlife conservation programs.

Our Shared Responsibility

The people of Pennsylvania have a tremendous opportunity to model effective wildlife and habitat management, public education, and tourism management along with effective and creative problem solving of elk-related problems. As other states east of the Mississippi River consider the possibility of reintroducing elk, many of them are looking to the experience and wisdom of Pennsylvanians, since our state was one of the first with a successful experience with elk reintroduction. Pennsylvania's perspective on this issue covers close to a 90-year period.

During the twenty-first century, it is my hope that wise decisions will continue to be made as Pennsylvania continues to write its history in conservation and elk management. Such a work is not just the responsibility of a particular agency or of the people who live on the elk range. It is each citizen's opportunity and each citizen's responsibility.

What Can You Do for the Elk?

If you have developed a "heart for the herd," become involved in your community to educate people – young and old alike – about the elk in Pennsylvania. Presenting programs for community and school groups is one way to spread the word about elk and habitat conservation. Students can write research papers about the elk and wildlife management and responsible hunting. Teachers can integrate elk information and conservation into their curriculums, and arrange field trips to the elk range. Pamphlets and literature can be obtained by contacting the Rocky Mountain Elk Foundation (RMEF), the Pennsylvania Game Commission, or the local Tourist Bureau. Talking with your friends, family, and neighbors, and sharing elk photos and information are additional ways of generating interest and support for the elk. Bringing others along to see the elk can be a lot of fun as well.

Supporting agencies like the RMEF with financial contributions is another tangible and important way of helping the elk in Pennsylvania. The RMEF has already contributed more than two million dollars to support elk habitat enhancement and land acquisition for the Pennsylvania elk range. Its members are people like you and I who care about the elk and their future and who are willing to give their financial support to a worthwhile program. Such support will enable our generation as well as future generations to enjoy the elk herd in Pennsylvania for many years to come.

Conservation by Choice, Not by Chance

During the past two decades, the results of conservation strategies and habitat improvements have been phenomenally successful in revitalizing the herd and increasing the elk population in Pennsylvania. Conservation efforts have required a lot of cooperative planning, hard work, research, negotiation, and financial support. Those who work for the agencies involved often have thankless jobs for ongoing work that deserves to be appreciated and acknowledged.

Although the prognosis on the elk herd seems very good at the present time, elk history in Pennsylvania has had some very sobering chapters. Perhaps that is why state residents and visitors alike, with the understandable exception of farmers and local residents who have suffered crop and vegetation losses, cherish and appreciate the Pennsylvania elk herd of today which has flourished to a population of more than 700.

Many visitors to the elk range know the history and have witnessed the reestablishment of the elk herd under sound conservation and wildlife management principles and practices in recent decades. Even people who are learning about the elk for the first time can appreciate the significance of the survival and the very existence of this magnificent herd of elk in the heart of the Pennsylvania state game lands, parks, and forests. Conservation of our precious natural resources is not by chance — it is by choice. The future of the Pennsylvania elk will be secure only as more and more people recognize the importance of managing the land and the elk herd responsibly for future generations to enjoy, and only as we choose to continue this important work in the twenty-first century.

Works Cited

"Anatomy of the Elk." *About the Elk.* The Hunting.Network. 15 Sept.
2001. *<http://www.elkhunting.com/about/anatomy1.asp>.*

Bishop, Jodi, compiled. "Elk Facts." *Kids & Teachers.* Rocky Mountain Elk
Foundation. 16 Oct. 2000 *<http://www.rmef.org/facts.htm>.*

Cogan, Rawland D. "2001 Elk Survey." *Pennsylvania Game News.* 72.4
(2001): 16-17.

—-. "Elk Calf Survival in Pennsylvania." *Elk in Pennsylvania.*
17 Jan. 2001. Pennsylvania Game Commission. 27 June 2001
<http://sites.state.pa.us/PA_Exec/PGC/elk/survival.htm>.

—-. "Modern Day Elk Hunt Approved." *Pennsylvania Game News.* 72.6
(2001): 15-17.

Cogan, Rawland D., Robert Cordes & Jon DeBerti. "Pennsylvania's Elk
Trap and Transfer Project." *Elk in Pennsylvania.* 29 May 2001.
Pennsylvania Game Commission. 27 June 2001
<http://sites.state.pa.us/PA_Exec/PGC/elk/elkArticl1.htm>.

"Elk Habitat." From "Habits and Habitats," *Bugle* Fall 1992. Rocky
Mountain Elk Foundation. 16 Oct. 2000.
<http://www.rmef.org/elknaturalhistory.html?main=/visitor.htm>.

"Elk in History." *Elk Natural History.* Rocky Mountain Elk Foundation.
16 Oct. 2000 *<http://www.rmef.org/elknaturalhistory.*
html?main=/visitor.htm>.

"Elk Mortalities 1975-99." *Elk Statistical Data,* 19 Jan. 2001. Pennsylvania
Game Commission. 2 Aug. 2001.
<http://sites.state.pa.us/PA_Exec/PGC/elk/mortal.htm>.

"Elk Wildlife Note." *Elk in Pennsylvania.* 17 Jan. 2001. Pennsylvania
Game Commission. 27 June 2001
<http://sites.state.pa.us/PA_Exec/PGC/pubs/w_notes/elk.htm>.

"Fast Facts About Elk." *Elk Natural History.* Rocky Mountain Elk
Foundation. 16 Oct. 2000
<http://www.rmef.org/elknaturalhistory.html?main=/visitor.htm>.

Furtman, Michael. *Seasons of the Elk*. Minoqua: NorthWord Press,
    Inc., 1997.

Geist, Valerius. *Elk Country*. Minocqua: NorthWord Press, Inc., 1991.

Harrison, Ralph. *The Elk of Pennsylvania*. Mechanicsburg: The
    Pennsylvania Forestry Association, 1995.

Jones, Larry. *The Challenge of His Call*. Revised 1999. Middleton, ID: CHJ
    Publishing, 1999.

Kosak, Joe. "History of the Pennsylvania Elk." *Elk in Pennsylvania*.
    17 Jan. 2001. Pennsylvania Game Commission. 27 June 2001.
    <http://sites.state.pa.us/PA_Exec/PGC/elk/history.htm>.

Knox, Jennifer. "Where Elk Came From." *Kids and Teachers*. Rocky
    Mountain Elk Foundation. 6 June 2001
    <http://www.rmef.org/kids_section.html?main=/wow.html>.

Krakel II, Dean. *Season of the Elk*. Kansas City, MO: The Lowell Press.
    1976.

Murie, Olaus J. *The Elk of North America*. Jackson: Teton Bookshop. 1979.

New Revised Standard Version Bible. New York: American Bible Society.
    1989.

"Pennsylvania Elk Watching and Nature Tourism Project." 9 May 2001.
    Fermata, Inc. 25 June 2001
    < http://www.fermatainc.com/pennelk/index.html>.

"Pennsylvania's Wildlife Conservation History, 1910-1919." Wildlife in
    Pennsylvania. 13 Jan. 2000. Pennsylvania Game Commission.
    2 Oct. 2000
    < http://sites.state.pa.us/PA_Exec/PGC/history/hstindex.htm>.

Petersen, David. *Among the Elk*. Flagstaff: Northland Publishing Co.
    1993.

Robb, Bob. *Elk Essentials*. Minnetonka: North American Hunting Club,
    1999.

"Visiting Pennsylvania's Elk Range." *Elk in Pennsylvania*. 17 Jan. 2001.
    Pennsylvania Game Commission. 27 June 2001
    <http://sites.state.pa.us/PA_Exec/PGC/elk/visit.htm>.

"Where are the Elk?" *All About Elk*. Rocky Mountain Elk Foundation.
    16 Oct. 2000
    <http://www.rmef.org/elknaturalhistory.html?main=/visitor.htm>.